Idaho Constitution

Table of Contents

PREAMBLE

We, the people of the State of Idaho,

grateful to Almighty God for our freedom,

to secure its blessings and promote

our common welfare do establish

this Constitution.

ARTICLE I – DECLARATION OF RIGHTS

SECTION 1. INALIENABLE RIGHTS OF MAN. All men are by nature free and equal, and have certain inalienable rights, among which are enjoying and defending life and liberty; acquiring, possessing and protecting property; pursuing happiness and securing safety.

SECTION 2. POLITICAL POWER INHERENT IN THE PEOPLE. All political power is inherent in the people. Government is instituted for their equal protection and benefit, and they have the right to alter, reform or abolish the same whenever they may deem it necessary; and no special privileges or immunities shall ever be granted that may not be altered, revoked, or repealed by the legislature.

SECTION 3. STATE INSEPARABLE PART OF UNION. The state of Idaho is an inseparable part of the American Union, and the Constitution of the United States is the supreme law of the land.

SECTION 4. GUARANTY OF RELIGIOUS LIBERTY. The exercise and enjoyment of religious faith and worship shall forever be guaranteed; and no person shall be denied any civil or political right, privilege, or capacity on account of his religious opinions; but the liberty of conscience hereby secured shall not be construed to dispense with oaths or affirmations, or excuse acts of licentiousness or justify polygamous or other pernicious practices, inconsistent with morality or the peace or safety of the state; nor to permit any person, organization, or association to directly or indirectly aid or abet, counsel or advise any person to commit the crime of bigamy or polygamy, or any other crime. No person shall be required to attend or support any ministry or place of worship, religious sect or denomination, or pay tithes against his consent; nor shall any preference be given by law to any religious denomination or mode of worship. Bigamy and polygamy are forever prohibited in the state, and the legislature shall provide by law for the punishment of such crimes.

SECTION 5. RIGHT OF HABEAS CORPUS. The privilege of the writ of habeas corpus shall not be suspended, unless in case of rebellion or invasion, the public safety requires it, and then only in such manner as shall be prescribed by law.

SECTION 6. RIGHT TO BAIL – CRUEL AND UNUSUAL PUNISHMENTS PROHIBITED. All persons shall be bailable by sufficient sureties, except for capital offenses, where the proof is evident or the presumption great. Excessive bail shall not be required, nor excess fines imposed, nor cruel and unusual punishments inflicted.

SECTION 7. RIGHT TO TRIAL BY JURY. The right of trial by jury shall remain inviolate; but in civil actions, three-fourths of the jury may render a verdict, and the legislature may provide that in all cases of misdemeanors five-sixths of the jury may render a verdict. A trial by jury may be waived in all criminal cases, by the consent of all parties, expressed in open court, and in civil actions by the consent of the parties, signified in such manner as may be prescribed by law. In civil actions the jury may consist of twelve or of any number less than twelve upon which the parties may agree in open court. Provided, that in cases of misdemeanor and in civil actions within the jurisdiction of any court inferior to the district court, whether such case or action be tried in such inferior court or in district court, the jury shall consist of not more than six.

SECTION 8. PROSECUTIONS ONLY BY INDICTMENT OR INFORMATION. No person shall be held to answer for any felony or criminal offense of any grade, unless on presentment or indictment of a grand jury or on information of the public prosecutor, after a commitment by a magistrate, except in cases of impeachment, in cases cognizable by probate courts or by justices of the peace, and in cases arising in the militia when in actual service in time of war or public danger; provided, that a grand jury may be summoned upon the order of the district court in the manner provided by law, and provided further, that after a charge has been ignored by a grand jury, no person shall be held to answer, or for trial therefor, upon information of public prosecutor.

SECTION 9. FREEDOM OF SPEECH. Every person may freely speak, write and publish on all subjects, being responsible for the abuse of that liberty.

SECTION 10. RIGHT OF ASSEMBLY. The people shall have the right to assemble in a peaceable manner, to consult for their common good; to instruct their representatives, and to petition the legislature for the redress of grievances.

SECTION 11. RIGHT TO KEEP AND BEAR ARMS. The people have the right to keep and bear arms, which right shall not be abridged; but this provision shall not prevent the passage of laws to govern the carrying of weapons concealed on the person nor prevent passage of legislation providing minimum sentences for crimes committed while in possession of a firearm, nor prevent the passage of legislation providing penalties for the possession of firearms by a convicted felon, nor prevent the passage of any legislation punishing the use of a firearm. No law shall impose licensure, registration or special taxation on the ownership or possession of firearms or ammunition. Nor shall any law permit the confiscation of firearms, except those actually used in the commission of a felony.

SECTION 12. MILITARY SUBORDINATE TO CIVIL POWER. The military shall be subordinate to the civil power; and no soldier in time of peace shall be quartered in any house without the consent of its owner, nor in time of war except in the manner prescribed by law.

SECTION 13. GUARANTIES IN CRIMINAL ACTIONS AND DUE PROCESS OF LAW. In all criminal prosecutions, the party accused shall have the right to a speedy and public trial; to have the process of the court to compel the attendance of witnesses in his behalf, and to appear and defend in person and with counsel. No person shall be twice put in jeopardy for the same offense; nor be compelled in any criminal case to be a witness against himself; nor be deprived of life, liberty or property without due process of law.

SECTION 14. RIGHT OF EMINENT DOMAIN. The necessary use of lands for the construction of reservoirs or storage basins, for the purpose of irrigation, or for rights of way for the construction of canals, ditches, flumes or pipes, to convey water to the place of use for any useful, beneficial or necessary purpose, or for drainage; or for the drainage of mines, or the working thereof, by means of roads, railroads, tramways, cuts, tunnels, shafts, hoisting works, dumps, or other necessary means to their complete development, or any other use necessary to the complete development of the material resources of the state, or the preservation of the health of its inhabitants, is hereby declared to be a public use, and subject to the regulation and control of the state. Private property may be taken for public use, but not until a just compensation, to be ascertained in the manner prescribed by law, shall be paid therefor.

SECTION 15. IMPRISONMENT FOR DEBT PROHIBITED. There shall be no imprisonment for debt in this state except in cases of fraud.

SECTION 16. BILLS OF ATTAINDER, ETC., PROHIBITED. No bill of attainder, ex post facto law, or law impairing the obligation of contracts shall ever be passed.

SECTION 17. UNREASONABLE SEARCHES AND SEIZURES PROHIBITED. The right of the people to be secure in their persons, houses, papers and effects against unreasonable searches and seizures shall not be violated; and no warrant shall issue without probable cause shown by affidavit, particularly describing the place to be searched and the person or thing to be seized.

SECTION 18. JUSTICE TO BE FREELY AND SPEEDILY ADMINISTERED. Courts of justice shall be open to every person, and a speedy remedy afforded for every injury of person, property or character, and right and justice shall be administered without sale, denial, delay, or prejudice.

SECTION 19. RIGHT OF SUFFRAGE GUARANTIED. No power, civil or military, shall at any time interfere with or prevent the free and lawful exercise of the right of suffrage.

SECTION 20. NO PROPERTY QUALIFICATION REQUIRED OF ELECTORS – EXCEPTIONS. No property qualifications shall ever be required for any person to vote or hold office except in school elections, or elections creating indebtedness, or in irrigation district elections, as to which last-named elections the legislature may restrict the voters to land owners.

SECTION 21. RESERVED RIGHTS NOT IMPAIRED. This enumeration of rights shall not be construed to impair or deny other rights retained by the people.

SECTION 22. RIGHTS OF CRIME VICTIMS. A crime victim, as defined by statute, has the following rights:

(1) To be treated with fairness, respect, dignity and privacy throughout the criminal justice process.
(2) To timely disposition of the case.
(3) To prior notification of trial court, appellate and parole proceedings and, upon request, to information about the sentence, incarceration and release of the defendant.
(4) To be present at all criminal justice proceedings.
(5) To communicate with the prosecution.
(6) To be heard, upon request, at all criminal justice proceedings considering a plea of guilty, sentencing, incarceration or release of the defendant, unless manifest injustice would result.

(7) To restitution, as provided by law, from the person committing the offense that caused the victim's loss.

(8) To refuse an interview, ex parte contact, or other request by the defendant, or any other person acting on behalf of the defendant, unless such request is authorized by law.

(9) To read presentence reports relating to the crime.

(10) To the same rights in juvenile proceedings, where the offense is a felony if committed by an adult, as guaranteed in this section, provided that access to the social history report shall be determined by statute.

Nothing in this section shall be construed to authorize a court to dismiss a case, to set aside or void a finding of guilt or an acceptance of a plea of guilty, or to obtain appellate, habeas corpus, or other relief from any criminal judgment, for a violation of the provisions of this section; nor be construed as creating a cause of action for money damages, costs or attorney fees against the state, a county, a municipality, any agency, instrumentality or person; nor be construed as limiting any rights for victims previously conferred by statute. This section shall be self-enacting. The legislature shall have the power to enact laws to define, implement, preserve, and expand the rights guaranteed to victims in the provisions of this section.

SECTION 23. THE RIGHTS TO HUNT, FISH AND TRAP. The rights to hunt, fish and trap, including by the use of traditional methods, are a valued part of the heritage of the State of Idaho and shall forever be preserved for the people and managed through the laws, rules and proclamations that preserve the future of hunting, fishing and trapping. Public hunting, fishing and trapping of wildlife shall be a preferred means of managing wildlife. The rights set forth herein do not create a right to trespass on private property, shall not affect rights to divert, appropriate and use water, or establish any minimum amount of water in any water body, shall not lead to a diminution of other private rights, and shall not prevent the suspension or revocation, pursuant to statute enacted by the Legislature, of an individual's hunting, fishing or trapping license.

ARTICLE II – DISTRIBUTION OF POWERS

SECTION 1. DEPARTMENTS OF GOVERNMENT. The powers of the government of this state are divided into three distinct departments, the legislative, executive and judicial; and no person or collection of persons charged with the exercise of powers properly belonging to one of these departments shall exercise any powers properly belonging to either of the others, except as in this constitution expressly directed or permitted.

ARTICLE III – LEGISLATIVE DEPARTMENT

SECTION 1. LEGISLATIVE POWER – ENACTING CLAUSE – REFERENDUM – INITIATIVE. The legislative power of the state shall be vested in a senate and house of representatives. The enacting clause of every bill shall be as follows: "Be it enacted by the Legislature of the State of Idaho."

The people reserve to themselves the power to approve or reject at the polls any act or measure passed by the legislature. This power is known as the referendum, and legal voters may, under such conditions and in such manner as may be provided by acts of the legislature, demand a referendum vote on any act or measure passed by the legislature and cause the same to be submitted to a vote of the people for their approval or rejection.

The people reserve to themselves the power to propose laws, and enact the same at the polls independent of the legislature. This power is known as the initiative, and legal voters may, under such conditions and in such manner as may be provided by acts of the legislature, initiate any desired legislation and cause the same to be submitted to the vote of the people at a general election for their approval or rejection.

SECTION 2. MEMBERSHIP OF HOUSE AND SENATE. (1) Following the decennial census of 1990 and in each legislature thereafter, the senate shall consist of not less than thirty nor more than thirty-five members. The legislature may fix the number of members of the house of representatives at not more than two times as many representatives as there are senators. The senators and representatives shall be chosen by the electors of the respective counties or districts into which the state may, from time to time, be divided by law.

(2) Whenever there is reason to reapportion the legislature or to provide for new congressional district boundaries in the state, or both, because of a new federal census or because of a decision of a court of competent jurisdiction, a commission for reapportionment shall be formed on order of the secretary of state. The commission shall be composed of six members. The leaders of the two largest political parties of each house of the legislature shall each designate one member and the state chairmen of the two largest political parties, determined by the vote cast for governor in the last gubernatorial election, shall each designate one member. In the event any appointing authority does not select the members within fifteen calendar days following the secretary of state's order to form the commission, such members shall be appointed by the Supreme Court. No member of the commission may be an elected or appointed official in the state of Idaho at the time of designation or selection.

(3) The legislature shall enact laws providing for the implementation of the provisions of this section, including terms of commission members, the method of filling vacancies on the commission, additional qualifications for commissioners and additional standards to govern the commission. The legislature shall appropriate funds to enable the commission to carry out its duties.

(4) Within ninety days after the commission has been organized or the necessary census data are available, whichever is later, the commission shall file a proposed plan for apportioning the senate and house of representatives of the legislature with the office of the secretary of state. At the same time, and with the same effect, the commission shall prepare and file a plan for congressional districts. Any final action of the commission on a proposed plan shall be approved by a vote of two-thirds of the members of the commission. All deliberations of the commission shall be open to the public.

(5) The legislative districts created by the commission shall be in effect for all elections held after the plan is filed and until a new plan is required and filed, unless amended by court order. The Supreme Court shall have original jurisdiction over actions involving challenges to legislative apportionment.

(6) A member of the commission shall be precluded from serving in either house of the legislature for five years following such member's service on the commission.

SECTION 3. TERM OF OFFICE. The senators and representatives shall be elected for the term of two (2) years, from and after the first day of December next following the general election.

SECTION 4. APPORTIONMENT OF LEGISLATURE. The members of the legislature following the decennial census of 1990 and each legislature thereafter shall be apportioned to not less than thirty nor more than thirty-five legislative districts of the state as may be provided by law.

SECTION 5. SENATORIAL AND REPRESENTATIVE DISTRICTS. A senatorial or representative district, when more than one county shall constitute the same, shall be composed of contiguous counties, and a county may be divided in creating districts only to the extent it is reasonably determined by statute that counties must be divided to create senatorial and representative districts which comply with the constitution of the United States. A county may be divided into more than one legislative district when districts are wholly contained within a single county. No floterial district shall be created. Multi-member districts may be created in any district composed of more than one county only to the extent that two representatives may be elected from a district from which one senator is elected. The provisions of this section shall apply to any apportionment adopted following the 1990 decennial census.

SECTION 6. QUALIFICATIONS OF MEMBERS. No person shall be a senator or representative who, at the time of his election, is not a citizen of the United States, and an elector of this state, nor anyone who has not been for one year next preceding his election an elector of the county or district whence he may be chosen.

SECTION 7. PRIVILEGE FROM ARREST. Senators and representatives in all cases, except for treason, felony, or breach of the peace, shall be privileged from arrest during the session of the legislature, and in going to and returning from the same, and shall not be liable to any civil process during the session of the legislature, nor during the ten days next before the commencement thereof; nor shall a member, for words uttered in debate in either house, be questioned in any other place.

SECTION 8. SESSIONS OF LEGISLATURE. The sessions of the legislature shall be held annually at the capital of the state, commencing on the second Monday of January of each year, unless a different day shall have been appointed by law, and at other times when convened by the governor.

SECTION 9. POWERS OF EACH HOUSE. Each house when assembled shall choose its own officers; judge of the election, qualifications and returns of its own members, determine its own rules of proceeding, and sit upon its own adjournments; but neither house shall, without the concurrence of the other, adjourn for more than three (3) days, nor to any other place than that in which it may be sitting.

SECTION 10. QUORUM, ADJOURNMENTS AND ORGANIZATION. A majority of each house shall constitute a quorum to do business; but a smaller number may adjourn from day to day, and may compel the attendance of absent members in such manner and under such penalties as such house may provide. A quorum being in attendance, if either house fail to effect an organization within the first four (4) days thereafter, the members of the house so failing shall be entitled to no compensation from the end of the said four (4) days until an organization shall have been effected.

SECTION 11. EXPULSION OF MEMBERS. Each house may, for good cause shown, with the concurrence of two-thirds (2/3) of all the members, expel a member.

SECTION 12. SECRET SESSIONS PROHIBITED. The business of each house, and of the committee of the whole shall be transacted openly and not in secret session.

SECTION 13. JOURNAL. Each house shall keep a journal of its proceedings; and the yeas and nays of the members of either house on any question shall at the request of any three (3) members present, be entered on the journal.

SECTION 14. ORIGIN AND AMENDMENT OF BILLS. Bills may originate in either house, but may be amended or rejected in the other, except that bills for raising revenue shall originate in the house of representatives.

SECTION 15. MANNER OF PASSING BILLS. No law shall be passed except by bill, nor shall any bill be put upon its final passage until the same, with the amendments thereto, shall have been printed for the use of the members; nor shall any bill become a law unless the same shall have been read on three several days in each house previous to the final vote thereon: provided, in case of urgency, two-thirds (2/3) of the house where such bill may be pending may, upon a vote of the yeas and nays, dispense with this provision. On the final passage of all bills, they shall be read at length, section by section, and the vote shall be by yeas and nays upon each bill separately, and shall be entered upon the journal; and no bill shall become a law without the concurrence of a majority of the members present.

SECTION 16. UNITY OF SUBJECT AND TITLE. Every act shall embrace but one subject and matters properly connected therewith, which subject shall be expressed in the title; but if any subject shall be embraced in an act which shall not be expressed in the title, such act shall be void only as to so much thereof as shall not be embraced in the title.

SECTION 17. TECHNICAL TERMS TO BE AVOIDED. Every act or joint resolution shall be plainly worded, avoiding as far as practicable the use of technical terms.

SECTION 18. AMENDMENTS TO BE PUBLISHED IN FULL. No act shall be revised or amended by mere reference to its title, but the section as amended shall be set forth and published at full length.

SECTION 19. LOCAL AND SPECIAL LAWS PROHIBITED. The legislature shall not pass local or special laws in any of the following enumerated cases, that is to say:

- Regulating the jurisdiction and duties of justices of the peace and constables.

- For the punishment of crimes and misdemeanors.

- Regulating the practice of the courts of justice.

- Providing for a change of venue in civil or criminal actions.

- Granting divorces.

- Changing the names of persons or places.

- Authorizing the laying out, opening, altering, maintaining, working on, or vacating roads, highways, streets, alleys, town plats, parks, cemeteries, or any public grounds not owned by the state.

- Summoning and impaneling grand and trial juries, and providing for their compensation.

- Regulating county and township business, or the election of county and township officers.

- For the assessment and collection of taxes.

- Providing for and conducting elections, or designating the place of voting.

- Affecting estates of deceased persons, minors, or other persons under legal disabilities.

- Extending the time for collection of taxes.

- Giving effect to invalid deeds, leases or other instruments.

- Refunding money paid into the state treasury.

- Releasing or extinguishing, in whole or in part, the indebtedness, liability or obligation of any person or corporation in this state, or any municipal corporation therein.

- Declaring any person of age, or authorizing any minor to sell, lease or incumber his or her property.

- Legalizing as against the state the unauthorized or invalid act of any officer.

- Exempting property from taxation.

- Changing county seats, unless the law authorizing the change shall require that two-thirds (2/3) of the legal votes cast at a general or special election shall designate the place to which the county seat shall be changed; provided, that the power to pass a special law shall cease as long as the legislature shall provide for such change by general law; provided further, that no special law shall be passed for any one county oftener than once in six (6) years.

- Restoring to citizenship persons convicted of infamous crimes.

- Regulating the interest on money.

- Authorizing the creation, extension or impairing of liens.

- Chartering or licensing ferries, bridges or roads.

- Remitting fines, penalties or forfeitures.

- Providing for the management of common schools.

- Creating offices or prescribing the powers and duties of officers in counties, cities, townships, election districts, or school districts, except as in this constitution otherwise provided.

- Changing the law of descent or succession.

- Authorizing the adoption or legitimization of children.

- For limitation of civil or criminal actions.

- Creating any corporation.

- Creating, increasing or decreasing fees, percentages, or allowances of public officers during the term for which said officers are elected or appointed.

SECTION 20. GAMBLING PROHIBITED. (1) Gambling is contrary to public policy and is strictly prohibited except for the following:

a. A state lottery which is authorized by the state if conducted in conformity with enabling legislation; and

b. Pari-mutuel betting if conducted in conformity with enabling legislation; and

c. Bingo and raffle games that are operated by qualified charitable organizations in the pursuit of charitable purposes if conducted in conformity with enabling legislation.

(2) No activities permitted by subsection (1) shall employ any form of casino gambling including, but not limited to, blackjack, craps, roulette, poker, bacarrat, keno and slot machines, or employ any electronic or electromechanical imitation or simulation of any form of casino gambling.

(3) The legislature shall provide by law penalties for violation of this section.

(4) Nowithstanding the foregoing, the following are not gambling and are not prohibited by this section:

a. Merchant promotional contests and drawings conducted incidentally to bona fide nongaming business operations, if prizes are awarded without consideration being charged to participants; and

b. Games that award only additional play.

SECTION 21. SIGNATURE OF BILL AND RESOLUTIONS. All bills or joint resolutions passed shall be signed by the presiding officers of the respective houses.

SECTION 22. WHEN ACTS TAKE EFFECT. No act shall take effect until sixty days from the end of the session at which the same shall have been passed, except in case of emergency, which emergency shall be declared in the preamble or in the body of the law.

SECTION 23. COMPENSATION OF MEMBERS. The legislature shall have no authority to establish the rate of its compensation and expense by law. There is hereby authorized the creation of the citizens committee on legislative compensation, which shall consist of six members, three to be appointed by the governor and three to be appointed by the supreme court, whose terms of office and qualifications shall be as provided by law. Members of the committee shall be citizens of the state of Idaho other than public officials holding an office to which compensation is attached. The committee shall, on or before the last day of November of each even-numbered year, establish the rate of compensation and expenses for services to be rendered by members of the legislature during the two-year period commencing on the first day of December of such year. The compensation and expenses so established shall, on or before such date, be filed with the secretary of state and the state controller. The rates thus established shall be the rates applicable for the two-year period specified unless prior to the twenty-fifth legislative day of the next regular session, by concurrent resolution, the senate and house of representatives shall reject or reduce such rates of compensation and expenses. In the event of rejection, the rates prevailing at the time of the previous session, shall remain in effect.

The officers of the legislature, including committee chairmen, may, by virtue of the office, receive additional compensation as may be provided by the committee. No change in the rate of compensation shall be made which applies to the legislature then in office except as provided herein.

When convened in extra session by the governor, no such session shall continue for a period longer than twenty days.

SECTION 24. PROMOTION OF TEMPERANCE AND MORALITY. The first concern of all good government is the virtue and sobriety of the people, and the purity of the home. The legislature should further all wise and well directed efforts for the promotion of temperance and morality.

SECTION 25. OATH OF OFFICE. The members of the legislature shall, before they enter upon the duties of their respective offices, take or subscribe the following oath or affirmation: "I do solemnly swear (or affirm, as the case may be) that I will support the constitution of the United States and the constitution of the state of Idaho, and that I will faithfully discharge the duties of senator (or representative, as the case may be) according to the best of my ability." And such oath may be administered by the governor, secretary of state, or judge of the Supreme Court, or presiding officer of either house.

SECTION 26. POWER AND AUTHORITY OVER INTOXICATING LIQUORS. From and after the thirty-first day of December in the year 1934, the legislature of the state of Idaho shall have full power and authority to permit, control and regulate or prohibit the manufacture, sale, keeping for sale, and transportation for sale, of intoxicating liquors for beverage purposes.

SECTION 27. CONTINUITY OF STATE AND LOCAL GOVERNMENTAL OPERATIONS. The legislature, in order to insure continuity of state and local governmental operations in periods of emergency resulting from disasters caused by enemy attack or in periods of emergency resulting from the imminent threat of such disasters, shall have the power and the immediate duty (1) to provide for prompt and temporary succession to the powers and duties of public offices, of whatever nature and whether filled by election or appointment, the incumbents of which may become unavailable for carrying on the powers and duties of such offices, and (2) to adopt such other measures as may be necessary and proper for so insuring the continuity of governmental operations. In the exercise of the powers hereby conferred, the legislature shall in all respects conform to the requirements of this constitution except to the extent that in the judgment of the legislature so to do would be impracticable or would admit of undue delay.

SECTION 28. MARRIAGE. A marriage between a man and a woman is the only domestic legal union that shall be valid or recognized in this state.

SECTION 29. LEGISLATIVE RESPONSE TO ADMINISTRATIVE RULES. The legislature may review any administrative rule to ensure it is consistent with the legislative intent of the statute that the rule was written to interpret, prescribe, implement or enforce. After that review, the legislature may approve or reject, in whole or in part, any rule as provided by law. Legislative approval or rejection of a rule is not subject to gubernatorial veto under section 10, article IV, of the constitution of the state of Idaho.

ARTICLE IV – EXECUTIVE DEPARTMENT

SECTION 1. EXECUTIVE OFFICERS LISTED – TERM OF OFFICE – PLACE OF RESIDENCE – DUTIES. The executive department shall consist of a governor, lieutenant governor, secretary of state, state controller, state treasurer, attorney general and superintendent of public instruction, each of whom shall hold his office for four years beginning on the first Monday in January next after his election, commencing with those elected in the year 1946, except as otherwise provided in this Constitution. The officers of the executive department shall, during their terms of office, reside within the state. Their official office shall be located in the county where the seat of government is located, there they shall keep the public records, books and papers. They shall perform such duties as are prescribed by this Constitution and as may be prescribed by law, provided that the state controller shall not perform any post-audit functions.

SECTION 2. ELECTION OF OFFICERS. The officers named in section 1 of this article shall be elected by the qualified electors of the state at the time and places of voting for members of the legislature, and the persons, respectively, having the highest number of votes for the office voted for shall be elected; but if two (2) or more shall have an equal and the highest number of votes for any one (1) of said offices, the two (2) houses of the legislature at its next regular session, shall forthwith, by joint ballot, elect one (1) of such persons for said office. The returns of election for the officers named in section 1 shall be made in such manner as may be prescribed by law, and all contested elections of the same, other than provided for in this section, shall be determined as may be prescribed by law.

SECTION 3. QUALIFICATIONS OF OFFICERS. No person shall be eligible to the office of governor or lieutenant governor unless he shall have attained the age of thirty years at the time of his election; nor to the office of secretary of state, state controller, or state treasurer, unless he shall have attained the age of twenty-five years; nor to the office of attorney general unless he shall have attained the age of thirty years, and have been admitted to practice in the Supreme Court of the state or territory of Idaho, and be in good standing at the time of his election. In addition to the qualifications above described each of the officers named shall be a citizen of the United States and shall have resided within the state or territory two years next preceding his election.

SECTION 4. GOVERNOR IS COMMANDER OF MILITIA. The governor shall be commander-in-chief of the military forces of the state, except when they shall be called into actual service of the United States. He shall have power to call out the militia to execute the laws, to suppress insurrection, or to repel invasion.

SECTION 5. SUPREME EXECUTIVE POWER VESTED IN GOVERNOR. The supreme executive power of the state is vested in the governor, who shall see that the laws are faithfully executed.

SECTION 6. GOVERNOR TO APPOINT OFFICERS. The governor shall nominate and, by and with the consent of the senate, appoint all officers whose offices are established by this constitution, or which may be created by law, and whose appointment or election is not otherwise provided for. If during the recess of the senate, a vacancy occurs in any state or district office, the governor shall appoint some fit person to discharge the duties thereof until the next meeting of the senate, when he shall nominate some person to fill such office. If the office of a justice of the supreme or district court, secretary of state, state controller, state treasurer, attorney general, or superintendent of public instruction shall be vacated by death, resignation or otherwise, it shall be the duty of the governor to fill the same by appointment, as provided by law, and the appointee shall hold his office until his successor shall be selected and qualified in such manner as may be provided by law.

SECTION 7. THE PARDONING POWER. Such board as may hereafter be created or provided by legislative enactment shall constitute a board to be known as the board of pardons. Said board, or a majority thereof, shall have power to remit fines and forfeitures, and, only as provided by statute, to grant commutations and pardons after conviction of a judgment, either absolutely or upon such conditions as they may impose in all cases of offenses against the state except treason or conviction on impeachment. The legislature shall by law prescribe the sessions of said board and the manner in which application shall be made, and regulated proceedings thereon, but no fine or forfeiture shall be remitted, and no commutation or pardon granted, except by the decision of a majority of said board, after a full hearing in open session, and until previous notice of the time and place of such hearing and the release applied for shall have been given by publication in some newspaper of general circulation at least once a week for four weeks. The proceedings and decision of the board shall be reduced to writing and with their reasons for their action in each case, and the dissent of any member who may disagree, signed by him, and filed, with all papers used upon the hearing, in the office of the secretary of state.

The governor shall have power to grant respites or reprieves in all cases of convictions for offenses against the state, except treason or conviction on impeachment, but such respites or reprievies [reprieves] shall not extend beyond the next session of the board of pardons; and such board shall at such session continue or determine such respite or reprieve, or they may commute or pardon the offense, as herein provided. In cases of conviction for treason the governor shall have the power to suspend the execution of the sentence until the case shall be reported to the legislature at its next regular session, when the legislature shall either pardon or commute the sentence, direct its execution, or grant a further reprieve.

SECTION 8. GOVERNOR MAY REQUIRE REPORTS – MESSAGES TO LEGISLATURE. The governor may require information in writing from the officers of the executive department upon any subject relating to the duties of their respective offices, which information shall be given upon oath whenever so required; he may also require information in writing, at any time under oath, from all offices and managers of state institutions, upon any subject relating to the condition, management and expenses of their respective offices and institutions, and may, at any time he deems it necessary, appoint a committee to investigate and report to him upon the condition of any executive office or state institution. The governor shall at the commencement of each session, and from time to time, by message, give to the legislature information of the condition of the state, and shall recommend such measures as he shall deem expedient. He shall also send to the legislature a statement, with vouchers, of the expenditures of all moneys belonging to the state and paid out by him. He shall also, at the commencement of each session, present estimates of the amount of money required to be raised by taxation for all purposes of the state.

SECTION 9. EXTRA SESSIONS OF LEGISLATURE. The governor may, on extraordinary occasions, convene the legislature by proclamation, stating the purposes for which he has convened it; but when so convened it shall have no power to legislate on any subjects other than those specified in the proclamation; but may provide for the expenses of the session and other matters incidental thereto. He may also, by proclamation, convene the senate in extraordinary session for the transaction of executive business.

SECTION 10. VETO POWER. Every bill passed by the legislature shall, before it becomes a law, be presented to the governor. If he approve, he shall sign it, and thereupon it shall become a law; but if he do not approve, he shall return it with his objections to the house in which it originated, which house shall enter the objections at large upon its journals and proceed to reconsider the bill. If then two-thirds (2/3) of the members present agree to pass the same, it shall be sent, together with the objections, to the other house, by which it shall likewise be reconsidered: and if approved by two-thirds (2/3) of the members present in that house, it shall become a law, notwithstanding the objections of the governor. In all such cases the vote of each house shall be determined by yeas and nays, to be entered on the journal. Any bill which shall not be returned by the governor to the legislature within five (5) days (Sundays excepted) after it shall have been presented to him, shall become a law in like manner as if he had signed it, unless the legislature shall, by adjournment, prevent its return, in which case it shall be filed, with his objections, in the office of the secretary of state within ten (10) days after such adjournment (Sundays excepted) or become a law.

SECTION 11. DISAPPROVAL OF APPROPRIATION BILLS. The governor shall have power to disapprove of any item or items of any bill making appropriations of money embracing distinct items, and the part or parts approved shall become a law and the item or items disapproved shall be void, unless enacted in the manner following: If the legislature be in session, he shall within five (5) days transmit to the house within which the bill originated a copy of the item or items thereof disapproved, together with his objections thereto, and the items objected to shall be separately reconsidered, and each item shall then take the same course as is prescribed for the passage of bills over the executive veto.

SECTION 12. LIEUTENANT GOVERNOR TO ACT AS GOVERNOR. In case of the failure to qualify, the impeachment, or conviction of treason, felony, or other infamous crime of the governor, or his death, removal from office, resignation, absence from the state, or inability to discharge the powers and duties of his office, the powers, duties and emoluments of the office for the residue of the term, or until the disability shall cease, shall devolve upon the lieutenant governor.

SECTION 13. LIEUTENANT GOVERNOR IS PRESIDENT OF SENATE. The lieutenant governor shall be president of the senate, but shall vote only when the senate is equally divided. In case of the absence or disqualification of the lieutenant governor from any cause which applies to the governor, or when he shall hold the office of governor, then the president pro tempore of the senate shall perform the duties of the lieutenant governor until the vacancy is filled or the disability removed.

SECTION 14. PRESIDENT PRO TEMPORE TO ACT AS GOVERNOR. In case of the failure to qualify in his office, death, resignation, absence from the state, impeachment, conviction of treason, felony or other infamous crime, or disqualification from any cause, of both governor and lieutenant governor, the duties of the governor shall devolve upon the president of the senate pro tempore, until such disqualification of either the governor or lieutenant governor be removed, or the vacancy filled; and if the president of the senate, for any of the above named causes, shall become incapable of performing the duties of governor, the same shall devolve upon the speaker of the house.

SECTION 15. GREAT SEAL OF THE STATE. There shall be a seal of this state, which shall be kept by the secretary of state and used by him officially, and shall be called "The great seal of the state of Idaho." The seal of the territory of Idaho, as now used, shall be the seal of the state until otherwise provided by law.

SECTION 16. GRANTS AND PERMISSIONS. All grants and permissions shall be in the name and by the authority of the state of Idaho, sealed with the great seal of the state, signed by the governor, and countersigned by the secretary of state.

SECTION 17. ACCOUNTS AND REPORTS OF OFFICERS. An account shall be kept by the officers of the executive department and of all public institutions of the state of all moneys received by them severally, from all sources, and for every service performed, and of all moneys disbursed by them severally, and a semi-annual report thereof shall be made to the governor, under oath; they shall also, at least twenty days preceding each regular session of the legislature, make full and complete reports of their official transactions to the governor, who shall transmit the same to the legislature.

SECTION 18. BOARD OF EXAMINERS. The governor, secretary of state, and attorney-general shall constitute a board of examiners, with power to examine all claims against the state, except salaries or compensation of officers fixed by law, and perform such other duties as may be prescribed by law: provided, that in the administration of moneys in cooperation with the federal government the legislature may prescribe any method of disbursement required to obtain the benefits of federal laws. And no claim against the state, except salaries and compensation of officers fixed by law, shall be passed upon by the legislature without first having been considered and acted upon by said board.

SECTION 19. SALARIES AND FEES OF OFFICERS. [Repealed]

SECTION 20. DEPARTMENTS LIMITED.All executive and administrative officers, agencies, and instrumentalities of the executive department of the state and their respective functions, powers, and duties, except for the office of governor, lieutenant governor, secretary of state, state controller, state treasurer, attorney general and superintendent of public instruction, shall be allocated by law among and within not more than twenty departments by no later than January 1, 1975. Subsequently, all new powers or functions shall be assigned to departments, divisions, sections or units in such a manner as will tend to provide an orderly arrangement in the administrative organization of state government. Temporary agencies may be established by law and need not be allocated within a department; however, such temporary agencies may not exist for longer than two years.

ARTICLE V – JUDICIAL DEPARTMENT

SECTION 1. FORMS OF ACTION ABOLISHED. The distinctions between actions at law and suits in equity, and the forms of all such actions and suits, are hereby prohibited; and there shall be in this state but one form of action for the enforcement or protection of private rights or the redress of private wrongs, which shall be denominated a civil action; and every action prosecuted by the people of the state as a party, against a person charged with a public offense, for the punishment of the same, shall be termed a criminal action.

Feigned issues are prohibited, and the fact at issue shall be tried by order of court before a jury.

SECTION 2. JUDICIAL POWER – WHERE VESTED. The judicial power of the state shall be vested in a court for the trial of impeachments, a Supreme Court, district courts, and such other courts inferior to the Supreme Court as established by the legislature. The courts shall constitute a unified and integrated judicial system for administration and supervision by the Supreme Court. The jurisdiction of such inferior courts shall be as prescribed by the legislature. Until provided by law, no changes shall be made in the jurisdiction or in the manner of the selection of judges of existing inferior courts.

SECTION 3. IMPEACHMENTS – WHERE AND HOW TRIED. The court for the trial of impeachments shall be the senate. A majority of the members elected shall be necessary to a quorum, and the judgment shall not extend beyond removal from, and disqualification to hold office in this state; but the party shall be liable to indictment and punishment according to law.

SECTION 4. IMPEACHMENTS – WHERE AND HOW TRIED – CONVICTION – IMPEACHMENT OF GOVERNOR. The house of representatives solely shall have the power of impeachment. No person shall be convicted without the concurrence of two-thirds (2/3) of the senators elected. When the governor is impeached, the chief justice shall preside.

SECTION 5. TREASON DEFINED AND LIMITED. Treason against the state shall consist only in levying war against it, or adhering to its enemies, giving them aid and comfort. No person shall be convicted of treason unless on the testimony of two witnesses to the same overt act, or on confession in open court. No conviction of treason or attainder shall work corruption of blood or forfeiture of estate.

SECTION 6. SUPREME COURT – NUMBER OF JUSTICES – TERM OF OFFICE – CALLING OF DISTRICT JUDGE TO SIT WITH COURT. The Supreme Court shall consist of five justices, a majority of whom shall be necessary to make a quorum or pronounce a decision. If a justice of the Supreme Court shall be disqualified from sitting in a cause before said court, or be unable to sit therein, by reason of illness or absence, the said court may call a district judge to sit in said court on the hearing of such cause.

The justices of the Supreme Court shall be elected by the electors of the state at large. The terms of office of the justices of the Supreme Court, except as in this article otherwise provided, shall be six years.

The justices of the Supreme Court shall, immediately after the first election under this constitution, be selected by lot, so that one shall hold his office for the term of two years, one for the term of four years, and one for the term of six years. The lots shall be drawn by the justices of the Supreme Court, who shall, for that purpose, assemble at the seat of government, and they shall cause the result thereof to be certified to by the secretary of state and filed in his office.

The chief justice shall be selected from among the justices of the Supreme Court by a majority vote of the justices. His term of office shall be four years. When a vacancy in the office of chief justice occurs, a chief justice shall be selected for a full four year term. The chief justice shall be the executive head of the judicial system.

SECTION 7. JUSTICES PROHIBITED FROM HOLDING OTHER OFFICES. No justice of the Supreme Court shall be eligible to any other office of trust or profit under the laws of this state during the term for which he was elected.

SECTION 8. TERMS OF SUPREME COURT. At least four (4) terms of the Supreme Court shall be held annually; two (2) terms at the seat of state government, and two (2) terms at the city of Lewiston, in Nez Perce county. In case of epidemic, pestilence, or destruction of court houses, the justices may hold the terms of the Supreme Court provided by this section at other convenient places, to be fixed by a majority of said justices. After six (6) years the legislature may alter the provisions of this section.

SECTION 9. ORIGINAL AND APPELLATE JURISDICTION OF SUPREME COURT. The Supreme Court shall have jurisdiction to review, upon appeal, any decision of the district courts, or the judges thereof, any order of the public utilities commission, any order of the industrial accident board, and any plan proposed by the commission for reapportionment created pursuant to section 2, article III; the legislature may provide conditions of appeal, scope of appeal, and procedure on appeal from orders of the public utilities commission, of the industrial accident board. On appeal from orders of the industrial accident board the court shall be limited to a review of questions of law. The Supreme Court shall also have original jurisdiction to issue writs of mandamus, certiorari, prohibition, and habeas corpus, and all writs necessary or proper to the complete exercise of its appellate jurisdiction.

SECTION 10. JURISDICTION OVER CLAIMS AGAINST THE STATE. The Supreme Court shall have original jurisdiction to hear claims against the state, but its decision shall be merely recommendatory; no process in the nature of execution shall issue thereon; they shall be reported to the next session of the legislature for its action.

SECTION 11. DISTRICT COURTS – JUDGES AND TERMS. The state shall be divided into five (5) judicial districts, for each of which a judge shall be chosen by the qualified electors thereof, whose term of office shall be four (4) years. And there shall be held a district court in each county, at least twice in each year, to continue for such time in each county as may be prescribed by law. But the legislature may reduce or increase the number of districts, district judges and district attorneys. This section shall not be construed to prevent the holding of special terms under such regulations as may be provided by law.

SECTION 12. RESIDENCE OF JUDGES – HOLDING COURT OUT OF DISTRICT – SERVICE BY RETIRED JUSTICES AND JUDGES. Every judge of the district court shall reside in the district for which he is elected. A judge of any district court, or any retired justice of the Supreme Court or any retired district judge, may hold a district court in any county at the request of the judge of the district court thereof, and upon the request of the governor, or of the chief justice, and when any such request is made or approved by the chief justice it shall be his duty to do so; but a cause in the district court may be tried by a judge pro tempore, who must be a member of the bar, agreed upon in writing by the parties litigant, or their attorneys of record, and sworn to try the cause. Any retired justice or district judge may sit with the Supreme Court and exercise the authority of a member thereof in any cause in which he is requested by that court so to do, and when requested by the chief justice shall perform such other duties pertaining to the judicial department of government as directed. Compensation for such service shall be as provided by the legislature.

SECTION 13. POWER OF LEGISLATURE RESPECTING COURTS. The legislature shall have no power to deprive the judicial department of any power or jurisdiction which rightly pertains to it as a coordinate department of the government; but the legislature shall provide a proper system of appeals, and regulate by law, when necessary, the methods of proceeding in the exercise of their powers of all the courts below the Supreme Court, so far as the same may be done without conflict with this Constitution, provided, however, that the legislature can provide mandatory minimum sentences for any crimes, and any sentence imposed shall be not less than the mandatory minimum sentence so provided. Any mandatory minimum sentence so imposed shall not be reduced.

SECTION 14. SPECIAL COURTS IN CITIES AND TOWNS. The legislature may provide for the establishment of special courts for the trial of misdemeanors in incorporated cities and towns, where the same may be necessary.

SECTION 15. CLERK OF SUPREME COURT. The clerk of the Supreme Court shall be appointed by the court, and shall hold his office during the pleasure of the court. He shall receive such compensation for his services as may be provided by law.

SECTION 16. CLERKS OF DISTRICT COURTS – ELECTION – TERM OF OFFICE. A clerk of the district court for each county shall be elected by the qualified voters thereof at the time and in the manner prescribed by law for the election of members of the legislature, and shall hold his office for the term of four (4) years.

SECTION 17. SALARIES OF JUSTICES AND JUDGES. The salary of the justices of the Supreme Court, the salary of judges of the court of appeals, the salary of the judges of the district court and the salary of magistrate judges shall be as provided by statute, and no justice of the Supreme Court, judge of the court of appeals, judge of the district court or magistrate judge, shall be paid his salary, or any part thereof, unless he shall have first taken and subscribed an oath that there is not in his hands any matter in controversy not decided by him which had been finally submitted for his consideration and determination, thirty days prior to the taking and subscribing such oath.

SECTION 18. PROSECUTING ATTORNEYS – TERM OF OFFICE – QUALIFICATIONS. A prosecuting attorney shall be elected for each organized county in the state, by the qualified electors of such county, and shall hold office for the term of two years, and commencing with the general election in 1984 shall hold office for the term of four years, and shall perform such duties as may be prescribed by law; he shall be a practicing attorney at law, and a resident and elector of the county for which he is elected. He shall receive such compensation for services as may be fixed by law.

SECTION 19. VACANCIES – HOW FILLED. All vacancies occurring in the offices provided for by this article of the Constitution shall be filled as provided by law.

SECTION 20. JURISDICTION OF DISTRICT COURT. The district court shall have original jurisdiction in all cases, both at law and in equity, and such appellate jurisdiction as may be conferred by law.

SECTION 21. JURISDICTION OF PROBATE COURTS. Repealed General Election November 6, 1962, HJR No. 10, Session 1961.

SECTION 22. JURISDICTION OF JUSTICES OF THE PEACE. Repealed General Election November 6, 1962, HJR No. 10, Session 1961.

SECTION 23. QUALIFICATIONS OF DISTRICT JUDGES. No person shall be eligible to the office of district judge unless he be learned in the law, thirty (30) years of age, and a citizen of the United States, and shall have resided in the state or territory at least two (2) years next preceding his election, nor unless he shall have been at the time of his election, an elector in the judicial district for which he is elected.

SECTION 24. JUDICIAL DISTRICTS ENUMERATED. Until otherwise provided by law, the judicial districts shall be five (5) in number, and constituted of the following counties, viz:

- First District – Shoshone and Kootenai.

- Second District – Latah, Nez Perce, and Idaho.

- Third District – Washington, Ada, Boise, and Owyhee.

- Fourth District – Cassia, Elmore, Logan, and Alturas.

- Fifth District – Bear Lake, Bingham, Oneida, Lemhi, and Custer.

SECTION 25. DEFECTS IN LAW TO BE REPORTED BY JUDGES. The judges of the district courts shall, on or before the first day of July in each year, report in writing to the justices of the Supreme Court, such defects or omissions in the laws as their knowledge and experience may suggest, and the justices of the Supreme Court shall, on or before the first day of December of each year, report in writing to the governor, to be by him transmitted to the legislature, together with his message, such defects and omissions in the Constitution and laws as they may find to exist.

SECTION 26. COURT PROCEDURE TO BE GENERAL AND UNIFORM. All laws relating to courts shall be general and of uniform operation throughout the state, and the organized judicial powers, proceedings, and practices of all the courts of the same class or grade, so far as regulated by law, and the force and effect of the proceedings, judgments, and decrees of such courts, severally, shall be uniform.

SECTION 27. CHANGE IN COMPENSATION OF OFFICERS. The legislature may by law diminish or increase the compensation of any or all of the following officers, to wit: governor, lieutenant governor, secretary of state, state controller, state treasurer, attorney general, superintendent of public instruction, justices of the Supreme Court, judges of the court of appeals and district courts and magistrate judges; but no diminution or increase shall affect the compensation of the officer then in office during his term, provided, however, that the legislature may provide for the payment of actual and necessary expenses of these officers incurred while in performance of official duty.

SECTION 28. REMOVAL OF JUDICIAL OFFICERS. Provisions for the retirement, discipline and removal from office of justices and judges shall be as provided by law.

ARTICLE VI – SUFFRAGE AND ELECTIONS

SECTION 1. SECRET BALLOT GUARANTEED. All elections by the people must be by ballot. An absolutely secret ballot is hereby guaranteed, and it shall be the duty of the legislature to enact such laws as shall carry this section into effect.

SECTION 2. QUALIFICATIONS OF ELECTORS. Every male or female citizen of the United States, eighteen years old, who has resided in this state, and in the county were [where] he or she offers to vote for the period of time provided by law, if registered as provided by law, is a qualified elector.

SECTION 3. DISQUALIFICATION OF CERTAIN PERSONS. No person is permitted to vote, serve as a juror, or hold any civil office who has, at any place, been convicted of a felony, and who has not been restored to the rights of citizenship, or who, at the time of such election, is confined in prison on conviction of a criminal offense.

SECTION 4. LEGISLATURE MAY PRESCRIBE ADDITIONAL QUALIFICATIONS. The legislature may prescribe qualifications, limitations, and conditions for the right of suffrage, additional to those prescribe [prescribed] in this article, but shall never annul any of the provisions in this article contained.

SECTION 5. RESIDENCE FOR VOTING PURPOSES NOT LOST OR GAINED. For the purpose of voting, no person shall be deemed to have gained or lost a residence by reason of his presence or absence while employed in the service of this state, or of the United States, nor while engaged in the navigation of the waters of this state or of the United States, nor while a student of any institution of learning, nor while kept at any alms house or other asylum at the public expense.

SECTION 6. RECALL OF OFFICERS AUTHORIZED. Every public officer in the state of Idaho, excepting the judicial officers, is subject to recall by the legal voters of the state or of the electoral district from which he is elected. The legislature shall pass the necessary laws to carry this provision into effect.

SECTION 7. NONPARTISAN SELECTION OF SUPREME AND DISTRICT JUDGES. The selection of justices of the Supreme Court and district judges shall be nonpartisan. The legislature shall provide for their nomination and election, but candidates for the offices of justice of the Supreme Court and district judge shall not be nominated nor endorsed by any political party and their names shall not appear on any political party ticket, nor be accompanied on the ballot by any political party designation.

ARTICLE VII – FINANCE AND REVENUE

SECTION 1. FISCAL YEAR. The fiscal year shall commence on the second Monday of January in each year, unless otherwise provided by law.

SECTION 2. REVENUE TO BE PROVIDED BY TAXATION. The legislature shall provide such revenue as may be needful, by levying a tax by valuation, so that every person or corporation shall pay a tax in proportion to the value of his, her, or its property, except as in this article hereinafter otherwise provided. The legislature may also impose a license tax, both upon natural persons and upon corporations, other than municipal, doing business in this state; also a per capita tax: provided, the legislature may exempt a limited amount of improvements upon land from taxation.

SECTION 3. PROPERTY TO BE DEFINED AND CLASSIFIED. The word "property" as herein used shall be defined and classified by law.

SECTION 4. PUBLIC PROPERTY EXEMPT FROM TAXATION. The property of the United States, except when taxation thereof is authorized by the United States, the state, counties, towns, cities, villages, school districts, and other municipal corporations and public libraries shall be exempt from taxation; provided, however, that unimproved real property owned or held by the department of fish and game may be subject to a fee in lieu of taxes if the fees are authorized by statute but not to exceed the property tax for the property at the time of acquisition by the department of fish and game, unless the tax for that class of property shall have been increased.

SECTION 5. TAXES TO BE UNIFORM – EXEMPTIONS. All taxes shall be uniform upon the same class of subjects within the territorial limits, of the authority levying the tax, and shall be levied and collected under general laws, which shall prescribe such regulations as shall secure a just valuation for taxation of all property, real and personal: provided, that the legislature may allow such exemptions from taxation from time to time as shall seem necessary and just, and all existing exemptions provided by the laws of the territory, shall continue until changed by the legislature of the state: provided further, that duplicate taxation of property for the same purpose during the same year, is hereby prohibited.

SECTION 6. MUNICIPAL CORPORATIONS TO IMPOSE THEIR OWN TAXES. The legislature shall not impose taxes for the purpose of any county, city, town, or other municipal corporation, but may by law invest in the corporate authorities thereof, respectively, the power to assess and collect taxes for all purposes of such corporation.

SECTION 7. STATE TAXES TO BE PAID IN FULL. All taxes levied for state purposes shall be paid into the state treasury, and no county, city, town, or other municipal corporation, the inhabitants thereof, nor the property therein, shall be released or discharged from their or its proportionate share of taxes to be levied for state purposes.

SECTION 8. CORPORATE PROPERTY MUST BE TAXED. The power to tax corporations or corporate property, both real and personal, shall never be relinquished or suspended, and all corporations in this state or doing business therein, shall be subject to taxation for state, county, school, municipal, and other purposes, on real and personal property owned or used by them, and not by this constitution exempted from taxation within the territorial limits of the authority levying the tax.

SECTION 9. MAXIMUM RATE OF TAXATION. The rate of taxation of real and personal property for state purposes shall never exceed ten (10) mills on each dollar of assessed valuation, unless a proposition to increase such rate, specifying the rate proposed and the time during which the same shall be levied, shall have been submitted to the people at a general election, and shall have received a majority of all the votes cast for and against it at such election.

SECTION 10. MAKING PROFIT FROM PUBLIC MONEY PROHIBITED. The making of profit, directly or indirectly, out of state, county, city, town, township or school district money, or using the same for any purpose not authorized by law, by any public officer, shall be deemed a felony, and shall be punished as provided by law.

SECTION 11. EXPENDITURE NOT TO EXCEED APPROPRIATION. No appropriation shall be made, nor any expenditure authorized by the legislature, whereby the expenditure of the state during any fiscal year shall exceed the total tax then provided for by law, and applicable to such appropriation or expenditure, unless the legislature making such appropriation shall provide for levying a sufficient tax, not exceeding the rates allowed in section nine of this article, to pay such appropriation or expenditure within such fiscal year. This provision shall not apply to appropriations or expenditures to suppress insurrection, defend the state, or assist in defending the United States in time of war.

SECTION 12. STATE TAX COMMISSION, MEMBERS, TERMS, APPOINTMENT, VACANCIES, DUTIES, POWERS – COUNTY BOARDS OF EQUALIZATION, DUTIES. There shall be a state tax commission consisting of four (4) members, not more than two (2) of whom shall belong to the same political party. The members of said commission shall be appointed by the governor, by and with the consent of the senate; the first commission to consist of one (1) commissioner appointed for a term of two (2) years, one commissioner appointed for a term of four (4) years and two (2) commissioners appointed for a term of six (6) years, and appointments thereafter to be for a term of six (6) years; each commissioner to serve until his successor is appointed and qualified. If during the recess of the senate a vacancy occurs in said commission, it shall be the duty of the governor to fill such vacancy by appointment, and the appointee shall hold office for the unexpired term of his predecessor. The duties heretofore imposed upon the state board of equalization by the Constitution and laws of this state shall be performed by the state tax commission and said commission shall have such other powers and perform such other duties as may be prescribed by law, including the supervision and coordination of the work of the several county boards of equalization. The board of county commissioners for the several counties of the state, shall constitute boards of equalization for their respective counties, whose duty it shall be to equalize the valuation of the taxable property in the county, under such rules and regulations of the state tax commission as shall be prescribed by law.

SECTION 13. MONEY – HOW DRAWN FROM TREASURY. No money shall be drawn from the treasury, but in pursuance of appropriations made by law.

SECTION 14. MONEY – HOW DRAWN FROM COUNTY TREASURIES. No money shall be drawn from the county treasuries except upon the warrant of a duly authorized officer, in such manner and form as shall be prescribed by the legislature.

SECTION 15. LEGISLATURE TO PROVIDE SYSTEM OF COUNTY FINANCE. The legislature shall provide by law, such a system of county finance, as shall cause the business of the several counties to be conducted on a cash basis. It shall also provide that whenever any county shall have any warrants outstanding and unpaid, for the payment of which there are no funds in the county treasury, the county commissioners, in addition to other taxes provided by law, shall levy a special tax, not to exceed ten (10) mills on the dollar, of taxable property, as shown by the last preceding assessment, for the creation of a special fund for the redemption of said warrants; and after the levy of such special tax, all warrants issued before such levy, shall be paid exclusively out of said fund. All moneys in the county treasury at the end of each fiscal year, not needed for current expenses, shall be transferred to said redemption fund.

SECTION 16. LEGISLATURE TO PASS NECESSARY LAWS. The legislature shall pass all laws necessary to carry out the provisions of this article.

SECTION 17. GASOLINE TAXES AND MOTOR VEHICLE REGISTRATION FEES TO BE EXPENDED ON HIGHWAYS. On and after July 1, 1941 the proceeds from the imposition of any tax on gasoline and like motor vehicle fuels sold or used to propel motor vehicles upon the highways of this state and from any tax or fee for the registration of motor vehicles, in excess of the necessary costs of collection and administration and any refund or credits authorized by law, shall be used exclusively for the construction, repair, maintenance and traffic supervision of the public highways of this state and the payment of the interest and principal of obligations incurred for said purposes; and no part of such revenues shall, by transfer of funds or otherwise, be diverted to any other purposes whatsoever.

SECTION 18. IDAHO MILLENNIUM PERMANENT ENDOWMENT FUND – IDAHO MILLENNIUM INCOME FUND – IDAHO MILLENNIUM FUND. There is hereby created in the state treasury an Idaho Millennium Permanent Endowment Fund. The fund shall consist of eighty percent of the moneys received each year by the state of Idaho on and after January 1, 2007, pursuant to the master settlement agreement entered into between tobacco product manufacturers and the state of Idaho, and any other moneys that may be appropriated or otherwise directed to the fund by the legislature, including other moneys or assets that the fund receives by bequest or private donation. The moneys received annually for deposit to the fund, including earnings, shall forever remain inviolate and intact. No portion of the permanent endowment fund shall ever be transferred to any other fund, or used, or appropriated, except as follows: each year, the state treasurer shall distribute five percent of the permanent endowment fund's average monthly fair market value for the first twelve months of the preceding twenty-four months, to the Idaho Millennium Income Fund, and provided, that such distribution shall not exceed the permanent endowment fund's fair market value on the first business day of July.

The Idaho Millennium Income Fund, which is hereby created in the state treasury, is subject to appropriation as provided by law, and shall consist of the distribution from the Idaho Millennium Permanent Endowment Fund and other moneys that may be appropriated or otherwise directed to the fund as provided by law.

The remaining twenty percent of the moneys received by the state of Idaho on and after January 1, 2007, pursuant to the master settlement agreement entered into between tobacco product manufacturers and the state of Idaho and the earnings thereon, shall be deposited to the Idaho Millennium Fund. The fund may consist of any other moneys that may be appropriated or otherwise directed to the fund by the legislature, including other moneys or assets that the fund receives by bequest or private donation. Moneys in the fund shall be allowed to accumulate, but shall not exceed a maximum limit as determined by law. Any amounts so accumulating in the Idaho Millennium Fund which exceed the maximum limit, shall be transferred, no less than once a year, to the Idaho Millennium Permanent Endowment Fund, and such moneys and earnings in the permanent endowment fund shall also remain inviolate and intact.

ARTICLE VIII – PUBLIC INDEBTEDNESS AND SUBSIDIES

SECTION 1. LIMITATION ON PUBLIC INDEBTEDNESS. The legislature shall not in any manner create any debt or debts, liability or liabilities, except in case of war, to repel an invasion, or suppress an insurrection, unless the same shall be authorized by law, for some single object or work, to be distinctly specified therein, which law shall provide ways and means, exclusive of loans, for the payment of the interest on such debt or liability as it falls due, and also for the payment and discharge of the principal of such debt or liability within twenty years of the time of the contracting thereof, and shall be irrepealable until the principal and interest thereon shall be paid and discharged. But no such law shall take effect until at a general election it shall have been submitted to the people, and shall have received a majority of all the votes cast for or against it at such election, and all moneys raised by the authority of such laws shall be applied only to specified objects therein stated or to the payment of the debt thereby created, and such law shall be published prior to the general election at which it is submitted to the people, in the same manner as amendments to this constitution are published. The legislature may at any time after the approval of such law, by the people, if no debts shall have been contracted in pursuance thereof, repeal the same.

This section shall not apply to liabilities incurred for ordinary operating expenses, nor shall it apply to debts or liabilities that are repaid by the end of the fiscal year. The debts or liabilities of the independent public bodies corporate and politic created by law and which have no power to levy taxes or obligate the general fund of the state are not debts or liabilities of the state of Idaho. The provisions of this section shall not make illegal those types of financial transactions that were legal on or before November 3, 1998.

SECTION 2. LOAN OF STATE'S CREDIT PROHIBITED – HOLDING STOCK IN CORPORATION PROHIBITED – DEVELOPMENT OF WATER POWER. (1) The credit of the state shall not, in any manner, be given, or loaned to, or in aid of any individual, association, municipality or corporation; nor shall the state directly or indirectly, become a stockholder in any association or corporation, provided, that the state itself may control and promote the development of the unused water power within this state.

(2) Notwithstanding the provisions of subsection (1), there is hereby created the public school guarantee fund which shall consist of funds provided by law to guarantee the debt of school districts in accordance with law. The state may guarantee the debt of school districts and may guarantee debt incurred to refund the school district debt. Any debt guaranty, the school district debt guaranteed thereby, or any borrowing of the state undertaken to facilitate the payments of the state's obligation under any debt guaranty shall not be included as a debt of the state for the purposes of the limitation of Section 1 of Article VIII. The legislature may provide by law that reimbursement to the state shall be obtained from moneys which otherwise would be used for the support of the educational programs of the school district which incurred the debt with respect to which a payment under the state's guaranty pursuant to this section was made.

SECTION 2A. MUNICIPAL BOND BANK AUTHORITY. (1) Notwithstanding the provisions of subsection (1) of Section 2 of Article VIII, the legislature may enact laws authorizing the state to establish a bond bank authority to purchase the bonds, notes or other obligations of a municipality issued or undertaken for any purpose authorized by law and to lend money to a municipality with such loans to be secured by bonds, notes or other obligations of the municipality issued or undertaken as authorized by law. To enable the authority to obtain funds to purchase municipal bonds, notes or other obligations or to make loans to municipalities, the legislature may enact laws authorizing the bond bank authority to:

(a) Issue revenue bonds, notes or other obligations payable from or secured by bonds, notes or other obligations of one or more municipalities;

(b) Pledge or otherwise obligate, for and in the name and on behalf of the state as its agent and instrumentality, specific funds or revenues of the state, as a source of payment or security for bonds, notes or other obligations issued by the authority, with such priority over other uses of such funds or revenues as the authority shall determine, in accordance with law, to be necessary or appropriate;

(c) Establish debt service reserve funds or other reserve funds;

(d) Obtain private credit enhancement for bonds, notes or other obligations issued by the authority;

(e) Establish a revolving loan program to purchase municipal bonds, notes or other obligations or to lend money to municipalities;

(f) Invest moneys held by the authority, as proceeds or to pay or secure bonds, notes or other obligations issued by the authority, in such securities or obligations as are described in the indenture, trust agreement or other instrument providing for the issuance of the bonds, notes or other obligations;

(g) Invest any moneys held by the authority, in excess of funds described in paragraph (f) of this subsection, in any securities or other obligations in which a trustee may invest as provided by law;

(h) Take any other actions and enter into such other contract and agreements as it may determine to be necessary or appropriate to accomplish the purposes of a bond bank authority or this section.

(2) To provide for the sale of municipal bonds, notes or other obligations to the authority and for the issuance of municipal bonds, notes or other obligations for purchase by the authority or as security for loans from the authority, the legislature may enact laws authorizing a municipality, in addition to any other powers municipalities may have, and without regard to the restrictions or requirements that might otherwise apply under the laws of this state, but subject to the requirements of Section 3 of Article VIII, and any other limitations imposed upon municipalities by the Constitution of the State of Idaho, to:

(a) Issue bonds, notes or other obligations for sale to or as security for loans received from the authority, with such interest rate, maturity, redemption, security, remedies and other terms as the municipality may agree with the authority;

(b) Levy and collect property taxes, fees, rates, charges and other assessments to pay or secure the bonds, notes or other obligations issued by the municipality for sale to or as security for loans received from the authority;

(c) Pledge and assign to the authority or its designee property taxes, fees, rates, charges and other assessments, and rights to enforce the collection and application thereof, to pay or secure the bonds, notes or other obligations issued by the municipality for sale to or as security for loans received from the authority;

(d) Take any other actions and enter into such other contracts and agreements as it may determine with the authority to be necessary or appropriate to accomplish the purposes of a bond bank authority or this section.

(3) The provisions of Section 1 and subsection (1) of Section 2 of Article VIII shall not be construed as a limitation upon the authority granted by this section and any debt or liability of the state arising as a result of the exercise of powers authorized by this section shall not be deemed a debt of the state for purposes of Section 1 of Article VIII. The provisions of this section are supplemental to and shall not be construed as a repeal of or limitation upon any authority of a municipality under Section 3 or 4 of Article VIII, or any other authority lawfully exercisable by a municipality under the Constitution and laws of this state, including, among others, any authority to issue general obligation bonds, revenue bonds or tax anticipation notes or to enter into contracts for or undertake other financial obligations.

(4) For purposes of this section, "municipality" shall include any county, city, municipal corporation, school district, irrigation district, sewer district, water district, highway district or other special purpose district or political subdivision of the state established by law.

SECTION 3. LIMITATIONS ON COUNTY AND MUNICIPAL INDEBTEDNESS. No county, city, board of education, or school district, or other subdivision of the state, shall incur any indebtedness, or liability, in any manner, or for any purpose, exceeding in that year, the income and revenue provided for it for such year, without the assent of two[-]thirds (2/3) of the qualified electors thereof voting at an election to be held for that purpose, nor unless, before or at the time of incurring such indebtedness, provisions shall be made for the collection of an annual tax sufficient to pay the interest on such indebtedness as it falls due, and also to constitute a sinking fund for the payment of the principal thereof, within thirty (30) years from the time of contracting the same. Any indebtedness or liability incurred contrary to this provision shall be void: Provided, that this section shall not be construed to apply to the ordinary and necessary expenses authorized by the general laws of the state and provided further that any city may own, purchase, construct, extend, or equip, within and without the corporate limits of such city, off street parking facilities, public recreation facilities, and air navigation facilities, and for the purpose of paying the cost thereof may, without regard to any limitation herein imposed, with the assent of two[-]thirds (2/3) of the qualified electors voting at an election to be held for that purpose, issue revenue bonds therefor, the principal and interest of which to be paid solely from revenue derived from rates and charges for the use of, and the service rendered by, such facilities as may be prescribed by law, and provided further, that any city or other political subdivision of the state may own, purchase, construct, extend, or equip, within and without the corporate limits of such city or political subdivision, water system, sewage collection systems, water treatment plants, sewage treatment plants, and may rehabilitate existing electrical generating facilities, and for the purpose of paying the cost thereof, may, without regard to any limitation herein imposed, with the assent of a majority of the qualified electors voting at an election to be held for that purpose, issue revenue bonds therefor, the principal and interest of which to be paid solely from revenue derived from rates and charges for the use of, and the service rendered by such systems, plants and facilities, as may be prescribed by law; and provided further that any port district, for the purpose of carrying into effect all or any of the powers now or hereafter granted to port districts by the laws of this state, may contract indebtedness and issue revenue bonds evidencing such indebtedness, without the necessity of the voters of the port district authorizing the same, such revenue bonds to be payable solely from all or such part of the revenues of the port district derived from any source whatsoever excepting only those revenues derived from ad valorem taxes, as the port commission thereof may determine, and such revenue bonds not to be in any manner or to any extent a general obligation of the port district issuing the same, nor a charge upon the ad valorem tax revenue of such port district.

SECTION 3A. ENVIRONMENTAL POLLUTION CONTROL REVENUE BONDS – ELECTION ON ISSUANCE. Counties of the state may in the manner prescribed by law issue revenue bonds for the purpose of acquiring, constructing, installing and equipping facilities designed for environmental pollution control, including the acquisition of all technological facilities and equipment necessary or convenient for pollution control, to be financed for, or to be sold, leased or otherwise disposed of to, persons, associations, or corporations other than municipal corporations or other political subdivisions; provided, that such revenue bonds are issued with the assent of a majority of the qualified electors of the county voting at an election to be called and held for that purpose; and provided further, that such revenue bonds shall not be secured by the full faith and credit or the taxing power of the state or of any political subdivision thereof. No provision of this constitution, including, but not limited to sections 3 and 4 of article VIII and section 4 of article XII, shall be construed as a limitation upon the authority granted under this section. Nothing herein contained shall authorize any county of the state to operate any industrial or commercial enterprise.

SECTION 3B. PORT DISTRICT FACILITIES AND PROJECTS – REVENUE BOND FINANCING. Port districts may acquire, construct, install, and equip facilities or projects to be financed for, or to be leased, sold or otherwise disposed of to persons, associations or corporations other than municipal corporations and may in the manner prescribed by law issue revenue bonds to finance the costs thereof; provided that any such revenue bonds shall be payable solely from charges, rents or payments derived from the facilities or projects financed thereby and shall not be secured by the full faith and credit or the taxing power of the port district, the state, or any other political subdivision. No provision of this Constitution, including, but not limited to Sections 3 and 4 of Article VIII and Section 4 of Article XII, shall be construed as a limitation upon the authority granted under this section.

SECTION 3C. HOSPITALS AND HEALTH SERVICES AUTHORIZED – ACTIVITIES AND FINANCING. Provided that no ad valorem tax revenues shall be used for activities authorized by this section, public hospitals, ancillary to their operations and in furtherance of health care needs in their service areas, may: (i) incur indebtedness or liability to purchase, contract, lease or construct or otherwise acquire facilities, equipment, technology and real property for health care operations as provided by law; (ii) acquire, construct, install and equip facilities or projects to be financed for, or to be leased, sold or otherwise disposed of to persons, associations or corporations other than municipal corporations and may, in the manner prescribed by law, finance the costs thereof; (iii) engage in shared services and other joint or cooperative ventures; (iv) enter into joint ventures and partnerships; (v) form or be a shareholder of corporations or a member of limited liability companies; (vi) have members of its governing body or its officers or administrators serve as directors, managers, officers or employees of any venture, association, partnership, corporation or limited liability company as authorized by this section; (vii) own interests in partnerships, corporations and limited liability companies. Any obligations incurred pursuant to this section shall be payable solely from charges, rent or payments derived from the existing facilities and the facilities or projects financed thereby and shall not be secured by the full faith and credit or the taxing power of the county, hospital taxing district, the state, or any other political subdivision; and provided further, that any county or public hospital taxing district contracting such indebtedness shall own its just proportion to the whole amount so invested. The authority granted by this section shall be exercised for the delivery of health care and related service and with the prior approval of the governing body of the county, hospital district or other governing body of a public hospital. No provisions of this Constitution including, but not limited to Sections 3 and 4 of Article VIII, and Section 4 of Article XII, shall be construed as a limitation upon the authority granted under this section.

SECTION 3D. MUNICIPAL ELECTRIC SYSTEMS – AUTHORIZED INDEBTEDNESS. Notwithstanding the limitations and requirements of Section 3, Article VIII, of the Constitution of the State of Idaho, any city owning a municipal electric system may:

(a) acquire, construct, install and equip electric generating, transmission and distribution facilities for the purpose of supplying electricity to customers located within the service area of each system established by law and for the purpose of paying the cost thereof, may issue revenue bonds with the assent of a majority of the qualified electors voting at an election held as provided by law; and

(b) incur indebtedness or liability under agreements to purchase, share, exchange or transmit wholesale electricity for the use and benefit of customers located within such service area; provided that any revenue bonds, indebtedness or liability shall be payable solely from the rates, charges or revenues derived from the municipal electric system and shall not be secured by the full faith and credit or the taxing power of the city, the state or any political subdivision.

SECTION 3E. AIRPORTS AND AIR NAVIGATION FACILITIES – AIRPORT RELATED PROJECTS – REVENUE AND SPECIAL FACILITY BOND FINANCING. Political subdivisions of the state and regional airport authorities as defined by law, if operating an airport, may acquire, construct, install, and equip land, facilities, buildings, projects or other property, which are hereby deemed to be for a public purpose, to be financed for, or to be leased, sold or otherwise disposed of to persons, associations or corporations, or to be held by the subdivision or regional airport authority, and may in the manner prescribed by law issue revenue and special facility bonds to finance the costs thereof; provided that any such bonds shall be payable solely from fees, charges, rents, payments, grants, or any other revenues derived from the airport or any of its facilities, structures, systems, or projects, or from any land, facilities, buildings, projects or other property financed by such bonds, and shall not be secured by the full faith and credit or the taxing power of the subdivision or regional airport authority. No provision of this constitution including, but not limited to, sections 3 and 4 of article VIII and section 4 of article XII, shall be construed as a limitation upon the authority granted under this section.

SECTION 4. COUNTY, ETC., NOT TO LOAN OR GIVE ITS CREDIT. No county, city, town, township, board of education, or school district, or other subdivision, shall lend, or pledge the credit or faith thereof directly or indirectly, in any manner, to, or in aid of any individual, association or corporation, for any amount or for any purpose whatever, or become responsible for any debt, contract or liability of any individual, association or corporation in or out of this state.

SECTION 5. SPECIAL REVENUE FINANCING. The legislature may enact laws authorizing the creation of public corporations by counties or cities to issue nonrecourse revenue bonds or other nonrecourse revenue obligations and to apply the proceeds thereof in the manner and for the purposes heretofore or hereafter authorized by law, subject to the following limitations:

Nonrecourse revenue bonds and other nonrecourse revenue obligations issued pursuant to this section shall be payable only from money or other property received as a result of projects financed by the nonrecourse revenue bonds or other nonrecourse revenue obligations and from money and other property received from private sources.

Nonrecourse revenue bonds and other nonrecourse revenue obligations issued pursuant to this section shall not be payable from or secured by any tax funds or governmental revenue or by all or part of the faith and credit of the state or any political subdivisions.

Nonrecourse revenue bonds or other nonrecourse revenue obligations issued pursuant to this section may be issued only if the issuer certifies that it reasonably believes that the interest paid on the bonds or obligations will be exempt from income taxation by the federal government.

Nonrecourse revenue bonds or other nonrecourse revenue obligations may only be used to finance industrial development facilities consisting of manufacturing, processing, production, assembly, warehousing, solid waste disposal, recreation and energy facilities, excluding facilities to transmit, distribute or produce electrical energy.

The counties or cities shall never exercise their respective attributes of sovereignty including, but not limited to, the power to tax, the power of eminent domain, and the police power on behalf of any industrial development project authorized pursuant to this section.

Sections 2, 3 and 4 of Article VIII shall not be construed as a limitation upon the authority granted by this section. The proceeds of revenue bonds and other revenue obligations issued pursuant to this section for the purpose of financing privately owned property or loans to private persons or corporations shall be subject to audit by the state but shall not otherwise be deemed to be public money or public property for purposes of this constitution. This section is supplemental to and shall not be construed as a repeal of or limitation on any other authority lawfully exercisable under the constitution and laws of this state, including, among other [others], any existing authority to issue revenue bonds.

ARTICLE IX – EDUCATION AND SCHOOL LANDS

SECTION 1. LEGISLATURE TO ESTABLISH SYSTEM OF FREE SCHOOLS. The stability of a republican form of government depending mainly upon the intelligence of the people, it shall be the duty of the legislature of Idaho, to establish and maintain a general, uniform and thorough system of public, free common schools.

SECTION 2. BOARD OF EDUCATION. The general supervision of the state educational institutions and public school system of the state of Idaho, shall be vested in a state board of education, the membership, powers and duties of which shall be prescribed by law. The state superintendent of public instruction shall be ex officio member of said board.

SECTION 3. PUBLIC SCHOOL PERMANENT ENDOWMENT FUND TO REMAIN INTACT. The public school permanent endowment fund of the state shall forever remain inviolate and intact; the earnings of the public school permanent endowment fund shall be deposited into the public school earnings reserve fund and distributed in the maintenance of the schools of the state, and among the counties and school districts of the state in such manner as may be prescribed by law. No part of the public school permanent endowment fund principal shall ever be transferred to any other fund, or used or appropriated except as herein provided. Funds shall not be appropriated by the legislature from the public school earnings reserve fund except as follows: the legislature may appropriate from the public school earnings reserve fund administrative costs incurred in managing the assets of the public school endowment including, but not limited to, real property and monetary assets. The state treasurer shall be the custodian of these funds, and the same shall be securely and profitably invested as may be by law directed. As defined and prescribed by law, the state shall supply losses to the public school permanent endowment fund, excepting losses on moneys allocated from the public school earnings reserve fund.

SECTION 4. PUBLIC SCHOOL PERMANENT ENDOWMENT FUND DEFINED. The public school permanent endowment fund of the state shall consist of the proceeds from the sale of such lands as have heretofore been granted, or may hereafter be granted, to the state by the general government, known as school lands, and those granted in lieu of such; lands acquired by gift or grant from any person or corporation under any law or grant of the general government; and of all other grants of land or money made to the state from the general government for general educational purposes, or where no other special purpose is indicated in such grant; all estates or distributive shares of estates that may escheat to the state; all unclaimed shares and dividends of any corporation incorporated under the laws of the state; and all other grants, gifts, devises, or bequests made to the state for general educational purposes; and amounts allocated from the public school earnings reserve fund. Provided however, that proceeds from the sale of school lands may be deposited into a land bank fund to be used to acquire other lands within the state for the benefit of endowment beneficiaries. If those proceeds are not used to acquire other lands within a time provided by the legislature, the proceeds shall be deposited into the public school permanent endowment fund along with any earnings on the proceeds.

SECTION 5. SECTARIAN APPROPRIATIONS PROHIBITED. Neither the legislature nor any county, city, town, township, school district, or other public corporation, shall ever make any appropriation, or pay from any public fund or moneys whatever, anything in aid of any church or sectarian or religious society, or for any sectarian or religious purpose, or to help support or sustain any school, academy, seminary, college, university or other literary or scientific institution, controlled by any church, sectarian or religious denomination whatsoever; nor shall any grant or donation of land, money or other personal property ever be made by the state, or any such public corporation, to any church or for any sectarian or religious purpose; provided, however, that a health facilities authority, as specifically authorized and empowered by law, may finance or refinance any private, not for profit, health facilities owned or operated by any church or sectarian religious society, through loans, leases, or other transactions.

SECTION 6. RELIGIOUS TEST AND TEACHING IN SCHOOL PROHIBITED. No religious test or qualification shall ever be required of any person as a condition of admission into any public educational institution of the state, either as teacher or student; and no teacher or student of any such institution shall ever be required to attend or participate in any religious service whatever. No sectarian or religious tenets or doctrines shall ever be taught in the public schools, nor shall any distinction or classification of pupils be made on account of race or color. No books, papers, tracts or documents of a political, sectarian or denominational character shall be used or introduced in any schools established under the provisions of this article, nor shall any teacher or any district receive any of the public school moneys in which the schools have not been taught in accordance with the provisions of this article.

SECTION 7. STATE BOARD OF LAND COMMISSIONERS. The governor, superintendent of public instruction, secretary of state, attorney general and state controller shall constitute the state board of land commissioners, who shall have the direction, control and disposition of the public lands of the state, under such regulations as may be prescribed by law.

SECTION 8. LOCATION AND DISPOSITION OF PUBLIC LANDS. It shall be the duty of the state board of land commissioners to provide for the location, protection, sale or rental of all the lands heretofore, or which may hereafter be granted to or acquired by the state by or from the general government, under such regulations as may be prescribed by law, and in such manner as will secure the maximum long term financial return to the institution to which granted or to the state if not specifically granted; provided, that no state lands shall be sold for less than the appraised price. No law shall ever be passed by the legislature granting any privileges to persons who may have settled upon any such public lands, subsequent to the survey thereof by the general government, by which the amount to be derived by the sale, or other disposition of such lands, shall be diminished, directly or indirectly. The legislature shall, at the earliest practicable period, provide by law that the general grants of land made by congress to the state shall be judiciously located and carefully preserved and held in trust, subject to disposal at public auction for the use and benefit of the respective object for which said grants of land were made, and the legislature shall provide for the sale of said lands from time to time and for the sale of timber on all state lands and for the faithful application of the proceeds thereof in accordance with the terms of said grants; provided, that not to exceed one hundred sections of state lands shall be sold in any one year, and to be sold in subdivisions of not to exceed three hundred and twenty acres of land to any one individual, company or corporation. The legislature shall have power to authorize the state board of land commissioners to exchange granted or acquired lands of the state on an equal value basis for other lands under agreement with the United States, local units of government, corporations, companies, individuals, or combinations thereof.

SECTION 9. COMPULSORY ATTENDANCE AT SCHOOLS. The legislature may require by law that every child shall attend the public schools of the state, throughout the period between the ages of six and eighteen years, unless educated by other means, as provided by law.

SECTION 10. STATE UNIVERSITY – LOCATION, REGENTS, TUITION, FEES AND LANDS. The location of the University of Idaho, as established by existing laws, is hereby confirmed. All the rights, immunities, franchises, and endowments, heretofore granted thereto by the territory of Idaho are hereby perpetuated unto the said university. The regents shall have the general supervision of the university, and the control and direction of all the funds of, and appropriations to, the university, under such regulations as may be prescribed by law. The regents may impose rates of tuition and fees on all students enrolled in the university as authorized by law. No university lands shall be sold for less than ten dollars per acre, and in subdivisions not to exceed one hundred and sixty acres, to any one person, company or corporation.

SECTION 11. INVESTING PERMANENT ENDOWMENT FUNDS. The permanent endowment funds other than funds arising from the disposition of university lands belonging to the state, may be invested in United States, state, county, city, village, or school district bonds or state warrants or other investments in which a trustee is authorized to invest pursuant to state law.

ARTICLE X – PUBLIC INSTITUTIONS

SECTION 1. STATE TO ESTABLISH AND SUPPORT INSTITUTIONS. Educational, reformatory, and penal institutions, and those for the benefit of the insane, blind, deaf and dumb, and such other institutions as the public good may require, shall be established and supported by the state in such manner as may be prescribed by law.

SECTION 2. SEAT OF GOVERNMENT. The seat of government of the state of Idaho shall be located at Boise City for twenty years from the admission of the state, after which time the legislature may provide for its relocation, by submitting the question to a vote of the electors of the state at some general election.

SECTION 3. SEAT OF GOVERNMENT – CHANGE IN LOCATION. The legislature may submit the question of the location of the seat of government to the qualified voters of the state at the general election, then next ensuing, and a majority of all the votes upon said question cast at said election shall be necessary to determine the location thereof. Said legislature shall also provide that in case there shall be no choice of location at said election, the question of choice between the two places for which the highest number of votes shall have been cast shall be submitted in like manner to the qualified electors of the state at the next general election.

SECTION 4. PROPERTY OF TERRITORY BECOMES PROPERTY OF STATE. All property and institutions of the territory, shall, upon the adoption of the constitution, become the property and institutions of the state of Idaho.

SECTION 5. STATE PRISONS – CONTROL OVER. The state legislature shall establish a nonpartisan board to be known as the state board of correction, and to consist of three (3) members appointed by the governor, one (1) member for two (2) years, one (1) member for four (4) years, and one (1) member for six (6) years. After the appointment of the first board the term of each member appointed shall be six (6) years. This board shall have the control, direction and management of the penitentiaries of the state, their employees and properties, and of adult felony probation and parole, with such compensation, powers, and duties as may be prescribed by law.

SECTION 6. DIRECTORS OF INSANE ASYLUM. [REPEALED].

SECTION 7. CHANGE IN LOCATION OF INSTITUTIONS. The legislature for sanitary reasons may cause the removal to more suitable localities of any of the institutions mentioned in section one of this article.

ARTICLE XI – CORPORATIONS, PUBLIC AND PRIVATE

SECTION 1. CERTAIN GRANTS AND CHARTERS INVALIDATED. All existing charters or grants of special or exclusive privileges, under which the corporations or grantees shall not have organized or commenced business in good faith at the time of the adoption of this Constitution, shall thereafter have no validity.

SECTION 2. SPECIAL CHARTERS PROHIBITED. No charter of incorporation shall be granted, extended, changed or amended by special law, except for such municipal, charitable, educational, penal, or reformatory corporations as are or may be, under the control of the state; but the legislature shall provide by general law for the organization of corporations hereafter to be created: provided, that any such general law shall be subject to future repeal or alteration by the legislature.

SECTION 3. REVOCATION AND ALTERATION OF CHARTERS. The legislature may provide by law for altering, revoking, or annulling any charter of incorporation, existing and revocable at the time of the adoption of this Constitution, in such manner, however, that no injustice shall be done to the corporators.

SECTION 4. CUMULATIVE VOTING. The Legislature shall not prohibit corporations from electing directors by cumulative voting.

SECTION 5. REGULATION AND CONTROL OF RAILROADS. All railroads shall be public highways, and all railroad, transportation, and express companies shall be common carriers, and subject to legislative control, and the legislature shall have power to regulate and control by law, the rates of charges for the transportation of passengers and freight by such companies or other common carriers, from one point to another in the state. Any association or corporation organized for the purpose, shall have the right to construct and operate a railroad between any designated points within this state, and to connect within or at the state line, with railroads of other states and territories. Every railroad company shall have the right with its road, to intersect, connect with, or cross any other railroad, under such regulations as may be prescribed by law, and upon making due compensation.

SECTION 6. EQUAL TRANSPORTATION RIGHTS GUARANTEED. All individuals, associations, and corporations, similarly situated, shall have equal rights to have persons or property transported on and over any railroad, transportation, or express route in this state, except that preference may be given to perishable property. No undue or unreasonable discrimination shall be made in charges or facilities for transportation of freight or passengers of the same class, by any railroad, or transportation, or express company, between persons or places within this state; but excursion or commutation tickets may be issued and sold at special rates, provided such rates are the same to all persons. No railroad, or transportation, or express company shall be allowed to charge, collect, or receive, under penalties which the legislature shall prescribe, any greater charge or toll for the transportation of freight or passengers, to any place or station upon its route or line, than it charges for the transportation of the same class of freight or passengers to any more distant place or station upon its route or line within this state. No railroad, express, or transportation company, nor any lessee, manager, or other employee thereof, shall give any preference to any individual, association, or corporation, in furnishing cars or motive power, or for the transportation of money or other express matter.

SECTION 7. ACCEPTANCE OF CONSTITUTION BY CORPORATIONS. No corporation other than municipal corporations in existence at the time of the adoption of this Constitution, shall have the benefit of any future legislation, without first filing in the office of the secretary of state an acceptance of the provisions of this Constitution in binding form.

SECTION 8. RIGHT OF EMINENT DOMAIN AND POLICE POWER RESERVED. The right of eminent domain shall never be abridged, nor so construed as to prevent the legislature from taking the property and franchises of incorporated companies, and subjecting them to public use, the same as the property of individuals; and the police powers of the state shall never be abridged or so construed as to permit corporations to conduct their business in such manner as to infringe the equal rights of individuals, or the general well being of the state.

SECTION 9. INCREASE IN CAPITAL STOCK. No corporation shall issue stocks or bonds, except for labor done, services performed, or money or property actually received; and all fictitious increase of stock or indebtedness shall be void. The stock of corporations shall not be increased except in pursuance of general law, nor without the consent of the persons, holding a majority of the stock of the class to be increased, first obtained at a meeting, held pursuant to such notice as is provided by the legislature.

SECTION 10. REGULATION OF FOREIGN CORPORATIONS. No foreign corporation shall do any business in this state without having one or more known places of business, and an authorized agent or agents in the same, upon whom process may be served; and no company or corporation formed under the laws of any other country, state, or territory, shall have or be allowed to exercise or enjoy, within this state any greater rights or privileges than those possessed or enjoyed by corporations of the same or similar character created under the laws of this state.

SECTION 11. CONSTRUCTING RAILROAD IN CITY OR TOWN. No street, or other railroad, shall be constructed within any city, town, or incorporated village without the consent of the local authorities having the control of the street or highway proposed to be occupied by such street or other railroad.

SECTION 12. RETROACTIVE LAWS FAVORING CORPORATIONS PROHIBITED. The legislature shall pass no law for the benefit of a railroad, or other corporation, or any individual, or association of individuals retroactive in its operation, or which imposes on the people of any county or municipal subdivision of the state, a new liability in respect to transactions or considerations already past.

SECTION 13. TELEGRAPH AND TELEPHONE COMPANIES. Any association or corporation, or the lessees or managers thereof, organized for the purpose, or any individual, shall have the right to construct and maintain lines of telegraph or telephone within this state, and connect the same with other lines; and the legislature shall by general law of uniform operation provide reasonable regulations to give full effect to this section.

SECTION 14. CONSOLIDATION OF CORPORATIONS WITH FOREIGN CORPORATIONS. If any railroad, telegraph, express, or other corporation, organized under any of the laws of this state, shall consolidate, bysale or otherwise, with any railroad, telegraph, express, or other corporation, organized under any of the laws of any other state or territory, or of the United States, the same shall not thereby become a foreign corporation, but the courts of this state shall retain jurisdiction over the part of the corporate property within the limits of the state in all matters that may arise, as if said consolidation had not taken place.

SECTION 15. TRANSFER OF FRANCHISES. The legislature shall not pass any law permitting the leasing or alienation of any franchise so as to release or relieve the franchise or property held thereunder from any of the liabilities of the lessor or grantor, or lessee or grantee, contracted or incurred in the operation, use, or enjoyment of such franchise, or any of its privileges.

SECTION 16. TERM "CORPORATION" DEFINED. The term "corporation" as used in this article, shall be held and construed to include all associations and joint stock companies having or exercising any of the powers or privileges of corporations not possessed by individuals or partnerships.

SECTION 17. LIABILITY OF STOCKHOLDERS – DUES. Dues from private corporations shall be secured by such means as may be prescribed by law, but in no case shall any stockholder be individually liable in any amount over or above the amount of stock owned by him.

SECTION 18. COMBINATIONS IN RESTRAINT OF TRADE PROHIBITED. That no incorporated company or any association of persons or stock company, in the state of Idaho, shall directly or indirectly combine or make any contract with any other incorporated company, foreign or domestic, through their stockholders or the trustees or assignees of such stockholders, or in any manner whatsoever, for the purpose of fixing the price or regulating the production of any article of commerce or of produce of the soil, or of consumption by the people; and that the legislature be required to pass laws for the enforcement thereof, by adequate penalties, to the extent, if necessary for that purpose, of the forfeiture of their property and franchise.

ARTICLE XII – CORPORATIONS, MUNICIPAL

SECTION 1. GENERAL LAWS FOR CITIES AND TOWNS. The legislature shall provide by general laws for the incorporation, organization and classification of the cities and towns, in proportion to the population, which laws may be altered, amended, or repealed by the general laws. Cities and towns heretofore incorporated, may become organized under such general laws, whenever a majority of the electors at a general election, shall so determine, under such provisions therefor as may be made by the legislature.

SECTION 2. LOCAL POLICE REGULATIONS AUTHORIZED. Any county or incorporated city or town may make and enforce, within its limits, all such local police, sanitary and other regulations as are not in conflict with its charter or with the general laws.

SECTION 3. STATE NOT TO ASSUME LOCAL INDEBTEDNESS. The state shall never assume the debts of any county, town, or other municipal corporation, unless such debts shall have been created to repel invasion, suppress insurrection or defend the state in war.

SECTION 4. MUNICIPAL CORPORATIONS NOT TO LOAN CREDIT. No county, town, city, or other municipal corporation, by vote of its citizens or otherwise, shall ever become a stockholder in any joint stock company, corporation or association whatever, or raise money for, or make donation or loan its credit to, or in aid of, any such company or association: provided, that cities and towns may contract indebtedness for school, water, sanitary and illuminating purposes: provided, that any city or town contracting such indebtedness shall own its just proportion of the property thus created and receive from any income arising therefrom, its proportion to the whole amount so invested.

ARTICLE XIII – IMMIGRATION AND LABOR

SECTION 1. BUREAU OF IMMIGRATION – COMMISSIONER. There shall be established a bureau of immigration, labor and statistics, which shall be under the charge of a commissioner of immigration, labor and statistics, who shall be appointed by the governor, by and with the consent of the senate. The commissioner shall hold his office for two years, and until his successor shall have been appointed and qualified, unless sooner removed. The commissioner shall collect information upon the subject of labor, its relation to capital, the hours of labor and the earnings of laboring men and women, and the means of promoting their material, social, intellectual and moral prosperity. The commissioner shall annually make a report in writing to the governor of the state of the information collected and collated by him, and containing such recommendations as he may deem calculated to promote the efficiency of the bureau.

SECTION 2. PROTECTION AND HOURS OF LABOR. Not more than eight (8) hours actual work shall constitute a lawful day's work, on all state and municipal works, and the legislature shall pass laws to provide for the health and safety of the employees in factories, smelters, mines and ore reduction works.

SECTION 3. RESTRICTIONS ON CONVICT LABOR. [Repealed].

SECTION 4. CHILD LABOR IN MINES PROHIBITED. The employment of children under the age of fourteen (14) years in underground mines is prohibited.

SECTION 5. ALIENS NOT TO BE EMPLOYED ON PUBLIC WORK. No person, not a citizen of the United States, or who has not declared his intention to become such, shall be employed upon, or in connection with, any state or municipal works.

SECTION 6. MECHANICS' LIENS TO BE PROVIDED. The legislature shall provide by proper legislation for giving to mechanics, laborers, and material men an adequate lien on the subject matter of their labor.

SECTION 7. BOARDS OF ARBITRATION. The legislature may establish boards of arbitration whose duty it shall be to hear and determine all differences and controversies between laborers and their employers which may be submitted to them in writing by all the parties. Such boards of arbitration shall possess all the powers and authority in respect to administering oaths, subpoenaing witnesses, and compelling their attendance, preserving order during the sittings of the board, punishing for contempt, and requiring the production of papers and writings, and all other powers and privileges, in their nature applicable, conferred by law on justices of the peace.

SECTION 8. DUTIES AND COMPENSATION OF COMMISSIONER. The commissioner of immigration, labor and statistics shall perform such duties and receive such compensation as may be prescribed by law.

ARTICLE XIV – MILITIA

SECTION 1. PERSONS SUBJECT TO MILITARY DUTY. All able-bodied male persons, residents of this state, between the ages of eighteen and forty-five years, shall be enrolled in the militia, and perform such military duty as may be required by law; but no person having conscientious scruples against bearing arms, shall be compelled to perform such duty in time of peace. Every person claiming such exemption from service, shall, in lieu thereof, pay into the school fund of the county of which he may be a resident, an equivalent in money, the amount and manner of payment to be fixed by law.

SECTION 2. LEGISLATURE TO PROVIDE FOR ENROLMENT OF MILITIA. The legislature shall provide by law for the enrolment, equipment and discipline of the militia, to conform as nearly as practicable to the regulations for the government of the armies of the United States, and pass such laws to promote volunteer organizations as may afford them effectual encouragement.

SECTION 3. SELECTION AND COMMISSION OF OFFICERS. All militia officers shall be commissioned by the governor, the manner of their selection to be provided by law, and may hold their commissions for such period of time as the legislature may provide.

SECTION 4. PRESERVATION OF RECORDS, BANNERS, AND RELICS. All military records, banners, and relics of the state, except when in lawful use, shall be preserved in the office of the adjutant general as an enduring memorial of the patriotism and valor of the soldiers of Idaho; and it shall be the duty of the legislature to provide by law for the safekeeping of the same.

SECTION 5. NATIONAL AND STATE FLAGS ONLY TO BE CARRIED. All military organizations under the laws of this state shall carry no other device, banner or flag, than that of the United States or the state of Idaho.

SECTION 6. IMPORTATION OF ARMED FORCES PROHIBITED. No armed police force, or detective agency, or armed body of men, shall ever be brought into this state for the suppression of domestic violence except upon the application of the legislature, or the executive, when the legislature can not be convened.

ARTICLE XV – WATER RIGHTS

SECTION 1. USE OF WATERS A PUBLIC USE. The use of all waters now appropriated, or that may hereafter be appropriated for sale, rental or distribution; also of all water originally appropriated for private use, but which after such appropriation has heretofore been, or may hereafter be sold, rented, or distributed, is hereby declared to be a public use, and subject to the regulations and control of the state in the manner prescribed by law.

SECTION 2. RIGHT TO COLLECT RATES A FRANCHISE. The right to collect rates or compensation for the use of water supplied to any county, city, or town, or water district, or the inhabitants thereof, is a franchise, and can not be exercised except by authority of and in the manner prescribed by law.

SECTION 3. WATER OF NATURAL STREAM – RIGHT TO APPROPRIATE – STATE'S REGULATORY POWER – PRIORITIES. The right to divert and appropriate the unappropriated waters of any natural stream to beneficial uses, shall never be denied, except that the state may regulate and limit the use thereof for power purposes. Priority of appropriation shall give the better right as between those using the water; but when the waters of any natural stream are not sufficient for the service of all those desiring the use of the same, those using the water for domestic purposes shall (subject to such limitations as may be prescribed by law) have the preference over those claiming for any other purpose; and those using the water for agricultural purposes shall have preference over those using the same for manufacturing purposes. And in any organized mining district those using the water for mining purposes or milling purposes connected with mining, shall have preference over those using the same for manufacturing or agricultural purposes. But the usage by such subsequent appropriators shall be subject to such provisions of law regulating the taking of private property for public and private use, as referred to in section 14 of article I of this Constitution.

SECTION 4. CONTINUING RIGHTS TO WATER GUARANTEED. Whenever any waters have been, or shall be, appropriated or used for agricultural purposes, under a sale, rental, or distribution thereof, such sale, rental, or distribution shall be deemed an exclusive dedication to such use; and whenever such waters so dedicated shall have once been sold, rented or distributed to any person who has settled upon or improved land for agricultural purposes with the view of receiving the benefit of such water under such dedication, such person, his heirs, executors, administrators, successors, or assigns, shall not thereafter, without his consent, be deprived of the annual use of the same, when needed for domestic purposes, or to irrigate the land so settled upon or improved, upon payment therefor, and compliance with such equitable terms and conditions as to the quantity used and times of use, as may be prescribed by law.

SECTION 5. PRIORITIES AND LIMITATIONS ON USE. Whenever more than one person has settled upon, or improved land with the view of receiving water for agricultural purposes, under a sale, rental, or distribution thereof, as in the last preceding section of this article provided, as among such persons, priority in time shall give superiority of right to the use of such water in the numerical order of such settlements or improvements; but whenever the supply of such water shall not be sufficient to meet the demands of all those desiring to use the same, such priority of right shall be subject to such reasonable limitations as to the quantity of water used and times of use as the legislature, having due regard both to such priority of right and the necessities of those subsequent in time of settlement or improvement, may by law prescribe.

SECTION 6. ESTABLISHMENT OF MAXIMUM RATES. The legislature shall provide by law, the manner in which reasonable maximum rates may be established to be charged for the use of water sold, rented, or distributed for any useful or beneficial purpose.

SECTION 7. STATE WATER RESOURCE AGENCY. There shall be constituted a Water Resource Agency, composed as the Legislature may now or hereafter prescribe, which shall have power to construct and operate water projects; to issue bonds, without state obligation, to be repaid from revenues of projects; to generate and wholesale hydroelectric power at the site of production; to appropriate public waters as trustee for Agency projects; to acquire, transfer and encumber title to real property for water projects and to have control and administrative authority over state lands required for water projects; all under such laws as may be prescribed by the Legislature. Additionally, the State Water Resource Agency shall have power to formulate and implement a state water plan for optimum development of water resources in the public interest. The Legislature of the State of Idaho shall have the authority to amend or reject the state water plan in a manner provided by law. Thereafter any change in the state water plan shall be submitted to the Legislature of the State of Idaho upon the first day of a regular session following the change and the change shall become effective unless amended or rejected by law within sixty days of its admission [submission] to the Legislature.

ARTICLE XVI – LIVESTOCK

SECTION 1. LAWS TO PROTECT LIVESTOCK. The legislature shall pass all necessary laws to provide for the protection of livestock against the introduction or spread of pleuro pneumonia, glanders, splenetic or Texas fever, and other infectious or contagious diseases. The legislature may also establish a system of quarantine or inspection and such other regulations as may be necessary for the protection of stock owners and most conducive to the stock interests within this state

ARTICLE XVII – STATE BOUNDARIES

SECTION 1. NAME AND BOUNDARIES OF STATE. The name of this state is Idaho, and its boundaries are as follows: Beginning at a point in the middle channel of the Snake river where the northern boundary of Oregon intersects the same; then follow down the channel of Snake river to a point opposite the mouth of the Kooskooskia or Clearwater river; thence due north to the forty-ninth parallel of latitude; thence east along that parallel to the thirty-ninth degree of longitude west of Washington; thence south along that degree of longitude to the crest of the Bitter Root mountains; thence southward along the crest of the Bitter Root mountains till its intersection with the Rocky mountains; thence southward along the crest of the Rocky mountains to the thirty-fourth degree of longitude west of Washington; thence south along that degree of longitude to the forty-second degree of north latitude; thence west along that parallel to the eastern boundary of the state of Oregon; thence north along that boundary to the place of beginning.

ARTICLE XVIII – COUNTY ORGANIZATION

SECTION 1. EXISTING COUNTIES RECOGNIZED. The several counties of the territory of Idaho, as they now exist, are hereby recognized as legal subdivisions of this state.

SECTION 2. REMOVAL OF COUNTY SEATS. No county seat shall be removed unless upon petition of a majority of the qualified electors of the county, and unless two-thirds (2/3) of the qualified electors of the county, voting on the proposition at a general election, shall vote in favor of such removal. A proposition of removal of the county seat shall not be submitted in the same county more than once in six (6) years, except as provided by existing laws. No person shall vote at any county seat election who has not resided in the county six (6) months, and in the precinct ninety (90) days.

SECTION 3. DIVISION OF COUNTIES. No county shall be divided unless a majority of the qualified electors of the territory proposed to be cut off, voting on the proposition at a general election, shall vote in favor of such division: provided, that this section shall not apply to the creation of new counties. No person shall vote at such election who has not been ninety (90) days a resident of the territory proposed to be annexed. When any part of a county is stricken off and attached to another county, the part stricken off shall be held to pay its ratable proportion of all then existing liabilities of the county from which it is taken.

SECTION 4. NEW COUNTIES – SIZE AND VALUATION. No new counties shall be established which shall reduce any county to an area of less than four hundred (400) square miles, nor the valuation of its taxable property to less than one million dollars ($1,000,000); nor shall any new county be formed which shall have an area of less than four hundred (400) square miles, and taxable property of less than one million dollars ($1,000,000), as shown by the last previous assessment.

SECTION 4A. CONSOLIDATION OF COUNTIES. Counties of the state of Idaho as they now exist, or may hereafter be created or exist, may be consolidated in such manner as shall be prescribed by law; provided, no county may be consolidated with another county, except upon approval of a two-thirds (2/3) majority vote in each county, of the qualified electors thereof voting upon the question, and the limitations and provisions of sections 2, 3 and 4 of Article XVIII of the Constitution of the state of Idaho shall have no application to the question of consolidating counties.

SECTION 5. SYSTEM OF COUNTY GOVERNMENT. The legislature shall establish, subject to the provisions of this article, a system of county governments which shall be uniform throughout the state; and by general laws shall provide for township or precinct organizations.

SECTION 6. COUNTY OFFICERS. The legislature by general and uniform laws shall, commencing with the general election in 1970, provide for the election biennially, in each of the several counties of the state, of county commissioners and a coroner and for the election of a sheriff and a county assessor and, a county treasurer, who is ex-officio public administrator, every four years in each of the several counties of the state. All taxes shall be collected by the officer or officers designated by law. The clerk of the district court shall be ex-officio auditor and recorder. No other county offices shall be established, but the legislature by general and uniform laws shall provide for such township, precinct and municipal officers as public convenience may require, and shall prescribe their duties, and fix their terms of office. The legislature shall provide for the strict accountability of county, township, precinct and municipal officers for all fees which may be collected by them, and for all public and municipal moneys which may be paid to them, or officially come into their possession. The county commissioners may employ counsel when necessary. The sheriff, county assessor, county treasurer, and ex-officio tax collector, auditor and recorder and clerk of the district court shall be empowered by the county commissioners to appoint such deputies and clerical assistants as the business of their office may require, said deputies and clerical assistants to receive such compensation as may be fixed by the county commissioners.

SECTION 7. COUNTY OFFICERS – SALARIES. All county officers and deputies when allowed, shall receive, as full compensation for their services, fixed annual salaries, to be paid monthly out of the county treasury, as other expenses are paid. All actual and necessary expenses incurred by any county officer or deputy in the performance of his official duties, shall be a legal charge against the county, and may be retained by him out of any fees which may come into his hands. All fees which may come into his hands from whatever source, over and above his actual and necessary expenses, shall be turned into the county treasury at the end of each quarter. He shall at the end of each quarter, file with the clerk of the board of county commissioners, a sworn statement, accompanied by proper vouchers, showing all expenses incurred and all fees received, which must be audited by the board as other accounts.

SECTION 8. COUNTY OFFICERS – HOW PAID. The compensation provided in section seven for the officers therein mentioned shall be paid by fees or commissions, or both, as prescribed by law. All fees and commissions received by such officers in excess of the maximum compensation per annum provided for each in section seven of this article shall be paid to the county treasurer for the use and benefit of the county. In case the fees received in any one year by any one of such officers shall not amount to the minimum compensation per annum therein provided, he shall be paid by the county a sum sufficient to make his aggregate annual compensation equal to such minimum compensation.

SECTION 9. COUNTY OFFICERS – LIABILITY FOR FEES. The neglect or refusal of any county officer or deputy to account for and pay into the county treasury any money received as fees or compensation, in excess of his actual and necessary expenses, incurred in the performance of his official duties, within ten (10) days after his quarterly settlement with the county shall be a felony, and the grade of the crime shall be embezzlement of public funds, and be punishable as provided for such offenses.

SECTION 10. BOARD OF COUNTY COMMISSIONERS. The board of county commissioners shall consist of three (3) members. Their terms of office shall be as follows: At the general election of 1936 two (2) members shall be elected for a term of two (2) years and one (1) member for a term of four (4) years; at each biennial election thereafter one (1) member shall be elected for a term of two (2) years and one (1) for a term of four (4) years. The legislature shall enact the necessary measures to put this provision into effect and in so doing shall allot such four (4) year term to each commissioner's election district or like subdivision of the county which may be provided by law, in rotation.

SECTION 11. DUTIES OF OFFICERS. County, township, and precinct officers shall perform such duties as shall be prescribed by law.

SECTION 12. OPTIONAL FORMS OF COUNTY GOVERNMENT. The legislature by general law may provide for optional forms of county government for counties, which shall be the exclusive optional forms of county government. No optional form of county government shall be operative in any county until it has been submitted to and approved by a majority of the electors voting thereon in the county affected at a general or special election as provided by law. The electorate at said election shall be allowed to vote on whether they shall retain their present form of county government or adopt any of the optional forms of county government. In the event an optional form shall be adopted, the question whether to return to the original form or any other optional form, may be placed at subsequent elections, but not more frequently than each four years. When an optional form of county government has been adopted, the provisions of this section supersede sections 5, 6 and 10 of this article and sections 16 and 18 of article V.

ARTICLE XIX – APPORTIONMENT

SECTION 1. SENATORIAL DISTRICTS. This article was superseded by the code provisions for legislative districts, Sections 67-201 – 67-204. As originally adopted, this section provided as follows:

SENATORIAL DISTRICTS. Until otherwise provided by law the apportionment of the two houses of the legislature shall be as follows:

- The first senatorial district shall consist of the county of Shoshone, and shall elect two senators.

- The second shall consist of the counties of Kootenai and Latah, and shall elect one senator.

- The third shall consist of the counties of Nez Perce and Idaho, and shall elect one senator.

- The fourth shall consist of the counties of Nez Perce and Latah, and shall elect one senator.

- The fifth shall consist of the county of Latah, and shall elect one senator.

- The sixth shall consist of the county of Boise, and shall elect one senator.

- The seventh shall consist of the county of Custer, and shall elect one senator.

- The eighth shall consist of the county of Lemhi, and shall elect one senator.

- The ninth shall consist of the county of Logan, and shall elect one senator.

- The tenth shall consist of the county of Bingham, and shall elect one senator.

- The eleventh shall consist of the counties of Bear Lake, Oneida and Bingham, and shall elect one senator.

- The twelfth shall consist of the counties of Owyhee and Cassia, and shall elect one senator.

- The thirteenth shall consist of the county of Elmore, and shall elect one senator.

- The fourteenth shall consist of the county of Alturas, and shall elect one senator.

- The fifteenth shall consist of the county of Ada, and shall elect two senators.

- The sixteenth shall consist of the county of Washington, and shall elect one senator.

SECTION 2. REPRESENTATIVE DISTRICTS. This article was superseded by the code provisions for legislative districts, Sections 67-201 – 67-204. As originally adopted, this section provided as follows:

REPRESENTATIVE DISTRICTS. The several counties shall elect the following members of the house of representatives:

- The county of Ada, three members.

- The counties of Ada and Elmore, one member.

- The county of Alturas, two members.

- The county of Boise, two members.

- The county of Bingham, three members.

- The county of Cassia, one member.

- The county of Custer, two members.

- The county of Elmore, one member.

- The county of Idaho, one member.

- The counties of Idaho and Nez Perce, one member.

- The county of Kootenai, one member.

- The county of Latah, two members.

- The counties of Kootenai and Latah, one member.

- The county of Logan, two members.

- The county of Lemhi, two members.

- The county of Nez Perce, one member.

- The county of Oneida, one member.

- The county of Owyhee, one member.

- The county of Shoshone, four members.

- The county of Washington, two members.

- The counties of Bingham, Logan and Alturas, one member.

ARTICLE XX – AMENDMENTS

SECTION 1. HOW AMENDMENTS MAY BE PROPOSED.Any amendment or amendments to this Constitution may be proposed in either branch of the legislature, and if the same shall be agreed to by two-thirds (2/3) of all the members of each of the two (2) houses, voting separately, such proposed amendment or amendments shall, with the yeas and nays thereon, be entered on their journals, and it shall be the duty of the legislature to submit such amendment or amendments to the electors of the state at the next general election, and cause the same to be published without delay for at least three (3) times in every newspaper qualified to publish legal notices as provided by law. Said publication shall provide the arguments proposing and opposing said amendment or amendments as provided by law, and if a majority of the electors shall ratify the same, such amendment or amendments shall become a part of this Constitution.

SECTION 2. SUBMISSION OF SEVERAL AMENDMENTS. If two (2) or more amendments are proposed, they shall be submitted in such manner that the electors shall vote for or against each of them separately.

SECTION 3. REVISION OR AMENDMENT BY CONVENTION. Whenever two-thirds (2/3) of the members elected to each branch of the legislature shall deem it necessary to call a convention to revise or amend this Constitution, they shall recommend to the electors to vote at the next general election, for or against a convention, and if a majority of all the electors voting at said election shall have voted for a convention, the legislature shall at the next session provide by law for calling the same; and such convention shall consist of a number of members, not less than double the number of the most numerous branch of the legislature.

SECTION 4. SUBMISSION OF REVISED CONSTITUTION TO PEOPLE. Any Constitution adopted by such convention, shall have no validity until it has been submitted to, and adopted by, the people.

ARTICLE XXI – SCHEDULE AND ORDINANCE

SECTION 1. JUDICIAL PROCEEDINGS CONTINUED. That no inconvenience may arise from a change of the territorial government to a permanent state government, it is declared that all writs, actions, prosecutions, claims, liabilities, and obligations against the territory of Idaho, of whatsoever nature and rights of individuals, and of bodies corporate, shall continue as if no change had taken place in this government; and all process which may, before the organization of the judicial department under this Constitution, be issued under the authority of the territory of Idaho, shall be as valid as if issued in the name of the state.

SECTION 2. LAWS CONTINUED IN FORCE. All laws now in force in the territory of Idaho which are not repugnant to this Constitution shall remain in force until they expire by their own limitation or be altered or repealed by the legislature.

SECTION 3. TERRITORIAL FINES AND FORFEITURES ACCRUE TO STATE. All fines, penalties, forfeitures, and escheats accruing to the territory of Idaho shall accrue to the use of the state.

SECTION 4. TERRITORIAL BONDS AND OBLIGATIONS PASS TO STATE. All recognizances, bonds, obligations, or other undertakings heretofore taken, or which may be taken before the organization of the judicial department under this Constitution, shall remain valid, and shall pass over to and may be prosecuted in the name of the state; and all bonds, obligations, or other undertakings executed by this territory, or to any other officer in his official capacity, shall pass over to the proper state authority, and to their successors in office for the uses therein respectively expressed, and may be sued for and recovered accordingly. All criminal prosecutions and penal actions which have arisen or which may arise before the organization of the judicial department under this Constitution, and which shall then be pending, may be prosecuted to judgment and execution in the name of the state.

SECTION 5. TERRITORIAL OFFICERS TO CONTINUE IN OFFICE. All officers, civil and military, now holding their offices and appointments in this territory under the authority of the United States, or under the authority of this territory, shall continue to hold and exercise their respective offices and appointments until suspended under this Constitution.

SECTION 6. SUBMISSION OF CONSTITUTION TO ELECTORS. This Constitution shall be submitted for adoption or rejection, to a vote of the electors qualified by the laws of this territory to vote at all elections, at an election to be held on the Tuesday after the first Monday in November, A.D. 1889. Said election shall be conducted in all respects in the same manner as provided by the laws of the territory for general election, and the returns thereof shall be made and canvassed in the same manner and by the same authority as provided in cases of such general elections, and abstracts of such returns duly certified shall be transmitted to the board of canvassers now provided by law for canvassing the returns of votes for delegate in congress. The said canvassing board shall canvass the votes so returned, and certify and declare the result of said election in the same manner, as is required by law for the election of said delegate.

At the said election the ballots shall be in the following form: For the Constitution: Yes. No.

And as a heading to each of said ballots shall be printed on each ballot, the following instructions to voters:

All persons who desire to vote for the Constitution, or any of the articles submitted to a separate vote, may erase the word "no."

All persons who desire to vote against the Constitution, or against any article submitted separately may erase the word "yes."

Any person may have printed or written on his ballot only the words, "For the Constitution," or "Against the Constitution," and such ballots shall be counted for or against the Constitution accordingly.

SECTION 7. WHEN CONSTITUTION TAKES EFFECT. This Constitution shall take effect and be in full force immediately upon the admission of the territory as a state.

SECTION 8. ELECTION PROCLAMATION TO BE ISSUED. Immediately upon the admission of the territory as a state, the governor of the territory, or in case of his absence or failure to act, the secretary of the territory, or in case of his absence or failure to act, the president of this convention, shall issue a proclamation, which shall be published, and a copy thereof mailed to the chairman of the board of county commissioners of each county, calling an election by the people of all state, district, county, township, and other officers, created and made elective by this Constitution, and fixing a day for such election, which shall not be less than forty (40) days after the date of such proclamation, nor more than ninety (90) days after the admission of the territory as a state.

SECTION 9. ELECTION TO BE ORDERED – CONDUCT OF ELECTION. The board of commissioners of the several counties shall thereupon order such election for said day, and shall cause notice thereof to be given, in the manner and for the length of time provided by the laws of the territory in cases of general elections for delegate to congress, and county and other officers. Every qualified elector of the territory, at the date of said election, shall be entitled to vote thereat. Said election shall be conducted in all respects in the same manner as provided by the laws of the territory for general elections, and the returns thereof shall be made and canvassed in the same manner and by the same authority as provided in cases of such general election; but returns for all state and district officers and members of the legislature, shall be made to the canvassing board hereinafter provided for.

SECTION 10. CANVASS OF ELECTION RETURNS. The governor, secretary, controller and attorney general of the territory, and the president of this convention, or a majority of them, shall constitute a board of canvassers to canvass the vote at such elections for all state and district officers and members of the legislature. The said board shall assemble at the seat of government of the territory on the thirtieth day after the date of such election (or on the following day if such day fall on Sunday) and proceed to canvass the votes for all state and district officers and members of the legislature, in the manner provided by the laws of the territory for canvassing the vote for delegates to congress, and they shall issue certificates of election to the persons found to be elected to said offices severally, and shall make and file with the secretary of the territory an abstract certified by them, of the number of votes cast for each person for each of said offices and the total number of votes cast in each county.

SECTION 11. CERTIFICATES OF ELECTION. The canvassing boards of the several counties shall issue certificates of election to the several persons found by them to have been elected to the several county and precinct offices.

SECTION 12. QUALIFICATIONS OF OFFICERS. All officers elected at such election shall, within thirty days after they have been declared elected, take the oath required by this Constitution and give the same bond required by the law of the territory to be given in case of like officers of the territory, district or county, and shall thereupon enter upon the duties of their respective offices; but the legislature may require by law all such officers to give other or further bonds as a condition of their continuance in office.

SECTION 13. TENURE OF OFFICE. All officers elected at said election, shall hold their offices until the legislature shall provide by law, in accordance with this Constitution, for the election of their successors, and until such successors shall be elected and qualified.

SECTION 14. CONVENTION OF FIRST LEGISLATURE. The governor-elect of the state, immediately upon his qualifying and entering upon the duties of his office, shall issue his proclamation convening the legislature of the state at the seat of government on a day to be named in said proclamation and which shall not be less than thirty (30) nor more than sixty (60) days after the date of such proclamation. Within ten (10) days after the organization of the legislature, both houses of the legislature shall then and there proceed to elect, as provided by law, two (2) senators of the United States for the state of Idaho. At said election, the two (2) persons who shall receive the majority of all votes cast by said senators and represenatives [representatives], shall be elected as such United States senators, shall be so declared by the presiding officers of said joint session. The presiding officers of the senate and house, shall issue a certificate to each of said senators, certifying his election, which certificates shall also be signed by the governor and attested by the secretary of state.

SECTION 15. LEGISLATURE TO PASS NECESSARY LAWS. The legislature shall pass all necessary laws to carry into effect the provisions of this Constitution.

SECTION 16. TRANSFER OF CASES TO STATE COURTS. Whenever any two (2) of the judges of the Supreme Court of the state, elected under the provisions of this Constitution, shall have qualified in their offices, the causes then pending in the Supreme Court of the territory, and the papers, records, and proceedings of said court, and the seal and other property pertaining thereto, shall pass into the jurisdiction and possession of the Supreme Court of the state; and until so superceded the Supreme Court of the territory and the judges thereof shall continue, with like powers and jurisdiction, as if this Constitution had not been adopted. Whenever the judge of the district court of any district elected under the provisions of this Constitution shall have qualified in office, the several causes then pending in the district court of the territory, within any county in such district, and the records, papers, and proceedings of said district court, and the seal and other property pertaining thereto, shall pass into the jurisdiction and possession of the district court of the state for such county; and until the district courts of this territory shall be superseded in the manner aforesaid the said district courts and the judges thereof shall continue with the same jurisdiction and power to be exercised in the same judicial districts respectively, as heretofore constituted under the laws of the territory.

SECTION 17. SEALS OF COURTS. Until otherwise provided by law, the seals now in use in the Supreme and district courts of this territory are hereby declared to be the seals of the Supreme and district courts, respectively, of the state.

SECTION 18. TRANSFER OF PROBATE MATTERS. Whenever this Constitution shall go into effect, the books, records, and papers, and proceedings of the probate court in each county, and all causes and matters of administration and other matters pending therein, shall pass into the jurisdiction and possession of the probate court of the same county of the state, and the said probate court shall proceed to final decree or judgment, order, or other determination in the said several matters and causes as the said probate court might have done as if this Constitution had not been adopted.

SECTION 19. RELIGIOUS FREEDOM GUARANTEED – DISCLAIMER OF TITLE TO INDIAN LANDS. It is ordained by the state of Idaho that perfect toleration of religious sentiment shall be secured, and no inhabitant of said state shall ever be molested in person or property on account of his or her mode of religious worship. And the people of the state of Idaho do agree and declare that we forever disclaim all right and title to the unappropriated public lands lying within the boundaries thereof, and to all lands lying within said limits owned or held by any Indians or Indian tribes; and until the title thereto shall have been extinguished by the United States, the same shall be subject to the disposition of the United States, and said Indian lands shall remain under the absolute jurisdiction and control of the congress of the United States; that the lands belonging to citizens of the United States, residing without the said state of Idaho, shall never be taxed at a higher rate than the lands belonging to the residents thereof. That no taxes shall be imposed by the state on the lands or property therein belonging to, or which may hereafter be purchased by, the United States, or reserved for its use. And the debts and liabilities of this territory shall be assumed and paid by the state of Idaho. That this ordinance shall be irrevocable, without the consent of the United States and the people of the state of Idaho.

SECTION 20. ADOPTION OF FEDERAL CONSTITUTION. That in behalf of the people of Idaho, we, in convention assembled, do adopt the Constitution of the United States.

SIGNATURES. Done in open convention at Boise City, in the territory of Idaho, this sixth day of August, in the year of our Lord, one thousand eight hundred and eighty-nine.

Wm. H. Clagett, PresidentJohn LewisGeo. AinslieWm. C. MaxeyW.C.B. AllenA.E. MayhewRobt. AndersonW.J. McConnellH. ArmstrongHenry MelderOrlando B. BattenJohn H. MyerFrank W. BeaneJohn T. MorganJas. H. BeattyA.B. MossJ.W. BallentineAaron F. ParkerA.D. BevanA.J. PierceHenry B. BlakeA.J. PinkhamFrederick CampbellJ.W. PoeFrank P. CavanahThos. PyeattA.S. ChaneyJas. W. ReidChas. A. ClarkW.D. RobbinsI.N. CostonWm. H. SavidgeJas. I. CrutcherAug. M. SinnottStephen S. GliddenJames M. ShoupJohn S. GrayDrew W. StandrodWm. W. HammellFrank SteunenbergH.S. HamptonHomer StullH.O. HarknessWillis SweetFrank HarrisSam F. TaylorSol. HasbrouckJ.L. UnderwoodC.M. HaysLycurgus VineyardW.B. HeyburnJ.S. WhittonJohn HoganEdgar WilsonJ.M. HoweW.W. WoodsE.S. JewellJohn LempG.W. KingN.I. AndrewsH.B. KinportSamuel J. PritchardJas. W. LamoreauxJ.W. Brigham

AMENDMENTS TO CONSTITUTION OF IDAHO

AMENDMENT No. 1, Art. XVIII, Sec. 6
Proposed 1893, S.L. page 224, substitute for H.J.R. 3 & 4; ratified November 6, 1894.

AMENDMENT No. 2, Art.VI, Sec. 2
Proposed 1895, S.L. page 232, S.J.R. 2; ratified November 3, 1896.

AMENDMENT No. 3, Art.V, Sec. 18
Proposed 1895, S.L. page 236, S.J.R. 5; ratified November 3, 1896.

AMENDMENT No. 4, Art. XVIII, Sec. 6
Proposed 1895, S.L. page 237, H.J.R. 10; ratified November 3, 1896.

AMENDMENT No. 5, Art. XVIII, Sec. 4
Proposed 1897, S.L. page 166, H.J.R. 8; ratified November 8, 1898.

AMENDMENT No. 6, Art. XVIII, Secs. 7 & 9
Proposed 1897, S.L. page 185, H.J.R. 10; ratified November 8, 1898, two questions both ratified.

AMENDMENT No. 7, Art. IX, Sec. 11
Proposed 1899, S.L. page 330; S.J.R. 12; ratified November 6, 1900

AMENDMENT No. 8, Art. XIII, Sec. 2
Proposed 1901, S.L. page 311, H.J.R. 2; ratified November 4, 1902.

AMENDMENT No. 9, Art. VII, Sec. 9
Proposed 1905, S.L. page 441, S.J.R. 6; ratified November 6, 1906.

AMENDMENT No. 10, Art. XVIII, Sec. 6
Proposed 1907, S.L. page 585, H.J.R. 10; ratified November 3, 1908.

AMENDMENT No. 11, Art. XVIII, Sec. 6
Proposed 1909, S.L. page 439, S.J.R. 6; ratified November 8, 1910, three separate questions all ratified.

AMENDMENT No. 12, Art.V, Sec. 6
Proposed 1909, S.L. page 441, S.J.R. 7; ratified November 8, 1910.

AMENDMENT No. 13, Art. VIII, Sec. 1
Proposed 1909, S.L. page 447, H.J.R. 3; ratified November 8, 1910.

AMENDMENT No. 14, Art. IX, Sec. 7
Proposed 1909, S.L. page 457, H.J.R. 15; ratified November 8, 1910.

AMENDMENT No. 15, Art. III, Sec. 1
Proposed 1911, S.L. page 786, S.J.R. 12; ratified November 5, 1912.

AMENDMENT No. 16, Art. III, Sec. 1
Proposed 1911, S.L. page 787, S.J.R. 13; ratified November 5, 1912.

AMENDMENT No. 17, Art. VIII, Sec. 1
Proposed 1911, S.L. page 787, S.J.R. 16; ratified November 5, 1912.

AMENDMENT No. 18, Art. III, Sec. 2
Proposed 1911, S.L. page 788, H.J.R. 13; ratified November 5, 1912.

AMENDMENT No. 19, Art. VI, Sec. 6 ADDED
Proposed 1911, S.L. page 790, H.J.R. 19; ratified November 5, 1912.

AMENDMENT No. 20, Art. XIII, Sec. 3 REPEALED
Proposed 1911, S.L. page 791, H.J.R. 24; ratified November 5, 1912.

AMENDMENT No. 21, Art. IX, Sec. 2
Proposed 1911, S.L. page 791; H.J.R. 30; ratified November 5, 1912.

AMENDMENT No. 22, Art. XVIII, Sec. 6
Proposed 1912, Special Session, S.L. page 53, S.J.R. 1; ratified November 5, 1912, two separate questions – both ratified.

AMENDMENT No. 23, Art. III, Sec. 26 ADDED
Proposed 1915, S.L. page 395, S.J.R. 1; ratified November 7, 1916.

AMENDMENT No. 24, Art.IX, Sec. 8
Proposed 1915, S.L. page 396, H.J.R. 3; ratified November 7, 1916.

AMENDMENT No. 25, Art.V, Sec. 6
Proposed 1919, S.L. page 618, H.J.R. 6; ratified November 2, 1920.

AMENDMENT No. 26, Art.V, Sec. 9
Proposed 1919, S.L. page 619, H.J.R. 8; ratified November 2, 1920.

AMENDMENT No. 27, Art.VIII, Sec. 2
Proposed 1919, S.L. page 622, H.J.R. 13; ratified November 2, 1920.

AMENDMENT No. 28, Art. IV, Sec. 19
Proposed 1927, S.L. page 586, H.J.R. 3; ratified November 6, 1928.

AMENDMENT No. 29, Art. XVIII, Sec. 7
Proposed 1927, S.L. page 586, H.J.R. 4; ratified November 6, 1928.

AMENDMENT No. 30, Art.V, Sec. 18
Proposed 1927, S.L. page 587, H.J.R. 7; ratified November 6, 1928.

AMENDMENT No. 31, Art. IX, Sec. 11
Proposed 1927, S.L. page 589, H.J.R. 10; ratified November 6, 1928.

AMENDMENT No. 32, Art. XVIII, Sec. 6
Proposed 1927, S.L. page 590, H.J.R. 11; ratified November 6, 1928.

AMENDMENT No. 33, Art. XV, Sec. 3
Proposed 1927, S.L. page 591, H.J.R. 13; ratified November 6, 1928.

AMENDMENT No. 34, Art. X, Sec. 6 REPEALED
Proposed 1929, S.L. page 693, H.J.R. 5; ratified November 4, 1930.

AMENDMENT No. 35, Art. XVIII, Sec. 4a ADDED
Proposed 1931, S.L. page 460, S.J.R. 3; ratified November 8, 1932.

AMENDMENT No. 36, Art. I, Sec. 20
Proposed 1931, S.L. page 462, H.J.R. 2; ratified November 8, 1932.

AMENDMENT No. 37, Art. I, Sec. 7
Proposed 1933, S.L. page 468, S.J.R. 1; ratified November 6, 1934.

AMENDMENT No. 38, Art.VI, Sec. 7 ADDED
Proposed 1933, S.L. page 469, S.J.R. 2; ratified November 6, 1934.

AMENDMENT No. 39, Art. III, Sec. 26
Proposed 1933, S.L. page 470, S.J.R. 5; ratified November 6, 1934.

AMENDMENT No. 40, Art. XVIII, Sec. 10
Proposed 1933, S.L. page 471, S.J.R. 7; ratified November 6, 1934.

AMENDMENT No. 41, Art. V, Sec. 9
Proposed 1935, S.L. page 377, H.J.R. 1; ratified November 3, 1936.

AMENDMENT No. 42, Art. IX, Sec. 8
Proposed 1935, Extra-Ord. Sess. S.L. page 185, S.J.R. 1; ratified November 3, 1936.

AMENDMENT No. 43, Art. IX, Sec. 11
Proposed 1939, S.L. page 670, S.J.R. 5; ratified November 5, 1940.

AMENDMENT No. 44, Art. IV, Sec. 18
Proposed 1939, S.L. page 671, S.J.R. 7; ratified November 5, 1940.

AMENDMENT No. 45, Art.VII, Sec. 17 ADDED
Proposed 1939, S.L. page 672, H.J.R. 3; ratified November 5, 1940.

AMENDMENT No. 46, Art.IX, Sec. 8
Proposed 1941, S.L. page 484, H.J.R. 3; ratified November 3, 1942.

AMENDMENT No. 47, Art. X, Sec. 5
Proposed 1941, S.L. page 485, S.J.R. 5; ratified November 3, 1942.

AMENDMENT No. 48, Art.IV, Sec 1
Proposed 1943, S.L. page 380, S.J.R. 1; ratified November 7, 1944.

AMENDMENT No. 49, Art.VII, Sec. 12
Proposed 1943, S.L. page 381, S.J.R. 3, ratified November 7, 1944.

AMENDMENT No. 50, Art. VII, Sec 4
Proposed 1943, S.L. page 383, S.J.R. 4; ratified November 7, 1944.

AMENDMENT No. 51, Art. IV, Sec. 7
Proposed 1945, S.L. page 400, S.J.R. 3, ratified November 5, 1946.

AMENDMENT No. 52, Art.IX, Sec. 11
Proposed 1945, S.L. page 402, S.J.R. 4, ratified November 5, 1946.

AMENDMENT No. 53, Art. IV, Sec. 18
Proposed 1945, S.L. page 398, H.J.R. 3; ratified November 5, 1946.

AMENDMENT No. 54, Art.III, Sec. 23
Proposed 1946, (2nd E.S.) S.L. page 8, H.J.R. 1; ratified November 5, 1946.

AMENDMENT No. 55, Art. XVIII, Sec. 6
Proposed 1947, S.L. page 906, S.J.R. 5; ratified November 2, 1948.

AMENDMENT No. 56, Art. IV, Sec. 3
Proposed 1947, S.L. page 908, S.J.R. 6; ratified November 2, 1948.

AMENDMENT No. 57, Art. VI, Sec. 3
Proposed 1949, S.L. page 597, H.J.R. 2; ratified November 7, 1950.

AMENDMENT No. 58, ArtVIII, Sec. 3
Proposed 1949, S.L. page 598, H.J.R. 9; ratified November 7, 1950.

AMENDMENT No. 59, Art.IX, Sec. 8
Proposed 1951, S.L. page 658, H.J.R. 6; ratified November 4, 1952.

AMENDMENT No. 60, Art.V, Sec. 21
Proposed 1955, S.L. page 669, S.J.R. 4; ratified November 6, 1956.

AMENDMENT No. 61, Art.V, Sec. 22
Proposed 1955, S.L. page 670, S.J.R. 5; ratified November 6, 1956.

AMENDMENT No. 62, Art.IV, Sec. 1
Proposed 1955, S.L. page 672, S.J.R. 6; ratified November 6, 1956.

AMENDMENT No. 63, Art.III, Sec. 27 ADDED
Proposed 1959, S.L. page 658, S.J.R. 4; ratified November 8, 1960.

AMENDMENT No. 64, Art. XVIII, Sec. 6
Proposed 1959, S.L. page 661, H.J.R. 9; ratified November 8, 1960.

AMENDMENT No. 65, Art. VI, Sec. 3
Proposed 1961, S.L. page 1073, S.J.R. 1; ratified November 6, 1962.

AMENDMENT No. 66, Art. VI, Sec. 2
Proposed 1961, S.L. page 1076, S.J.R. 6; ratified November 6, 1962.

AMENDMENT No. 67, Art. V, Secs. 2, 21, 22, Art. XVIII, Sec. 6
Proposed 1961, S.L. page 1077, H.J.R. 10; ratified November 6, 1962.

AMENDMENT No. 68, Art. XVIII, Sec. 6
Proposed 1963, S.L. page 1147, S.J.R. 6; ratified November 3, 1964.

AMENDMENT No. 69, Art. VIII, Sec. 3
Proposed 1963, S.L. page 1149, H.J.R. 5; ratified November 3, 1964.

AMENDMENT No. 70, Art. XV, Sec. 7 ADDED
Proposed 1964 (E.S.), S.L. page 22, S.J.R. 1; ratified November 3, 1964.

AMENDMENT No. 71, Art. I, Sec. 7
Proposed 1965, S.L. page 952, S.J.R. 6; ratified November 8, 1966.

AMENDMENT No. 72, Art.V, Sec. 12
Proposed 1965, S.L. page 953, S.J.R. 7; ratified November 8, 1966.

AMENDMENT No. 73, Art. XI, Sec. 9
Proposed 1965, S.L. page 958, H.J.R. 10; ratified November 8, 1966.

AMENDMENT No. 74, Art.VIII, Sec. 3
Proposed 1966 (2nd E.S.), 1967 S.L. page 66, S.J.R. 4; ratified November 8, 1966.

AMENDMENT No. 75, Art. III, Sec. 8
Proposed 1967, S.L. page 1574, H.J.R. 1; ratified November 5, 1968.

AMENDMENT No. 76, Art.IV, Sec. 6
Proposed 1967, S.L. page 1575, H.J.R. 4; ratified November 5, 1968.

AMENDMENT No. 77, Art. V, Sec. 28
Proposed 1967, S.L. page 1576, H.J.R. 5; ratified November 5, 1968.

AMENDMENT No. 78, Art. VIII, Sec. 3
Proposed 1967, S.L. page 1577, H.J.R. 7; ratified November 5, 1968.

AMENDMENT No. 79, Art. IX, Sec. 11
Proposed 1968 (2nd E.S.), S.L. page 69, S.J.R. 4; ratified November 5, 1968.

AMENDMENT No. 80, Art. XVIII, Sec. 6
Proposed 1969, S.L. page 1416, H.J.R. 3; ratified November 3, 1970.

AMENDMENT No. 81, Art. XVIII, Sec. 6
Proposed 1970, S.L. page 738, S.J.R. 121; ratified November 3, 1970.

AMENDMENT No. 82, Art.IX, Sec. 9
Proposed 1972, S.L. page 1244, S.J.R. 124 As Amended; ratified November 7, 1972.

AMENDMENT No. 83, Art. IV, Sec. 20
Proposed 1972, S.L. page 1245, S.J.R. 132; ratified November 7, 1972.

AMENDMENT No. 84, Art.XI, Sec. 4
Proposed 1972, S.L. page 1250, H.J.R. 63; ratified November 7, 1972.

AMENDMENT No. 85, Art. VIII, Sec. 3
Proposed 1972, S.L. page 1251, H.J.R. 73; ratified November 7, 1972.

AMENDMENT No. 86, Art.VIII, Sec. 3A
Proposed 1974, S.L. page 1888, S.J.R. 114; ratified November 5, 1974.

AMENDMENT No. 87, Art.XX, Sec. 1
Proposed 1974, S.L. page 1890, S.J.R. 118; ratified November 5, 1974.

AMENDMENT No. 88, Art. VIII, Sec. 3
Proposed 1976, S.L. page 1269, S.J.R. 109; ratified November 2, 1976.

AMENDMENT No. 89, Art. III, Sec. 23
Proposed 1976, S.L. page 1272, H.J.R. 6; ratified November 2, 1976.

AMENDMENT No. 90, Art. VIII, Sec. 3B ADDED
Proposed 1977, S.L. page 978, S.J.R. 102; ratified November 7, 1978.

AMENDMENT No. 91, Art. I, Sec. 11
Proposed 1978, S.L. page 1031, S.J.R. 116; ratified November 7, 1978.

AMENDMENT No. 92, Art.V, Sec. 13
Proposed 1978, S.L. page 1032; H.J.R. 6, As Amended; ratified November 7, 1978.

AMENDMENT No. 93, Art. III, Sec. 1
Proposed 1980, S.L. page 1028, S.J.R. 112, ratified November 4, 1980.

AMENDMENT No. 94, Art.IX, Sec. 5
Proposed 1980, S.L. page 1030, H.J.R. 12, As Amended, ratified November 4, 1980.

AMENDMENT No. 95, Art. V, Sec. 6
Proposed 1981, S.L. page 776, H.J.R. 2, ratified November 2, 1982.

AMENDMENT No. 96, Art. VI. Sec. 3
Proposed 1981, S.L. page 777, H.J.R. 7, ratified November 2, 1982.

AMENDMENT No. 97, Art. XI, Sec. 4
Proposed 1982, S.L. page 930, S.J.R. 110, ratified November 2, 1982.

AMENDMENT No. 98, Art. I, Sec. 7
Proposed 1982, S.L. page 931, S.J.R. 112, ratified November 2, 1982.

AMENDMENT No. 99, Art. VI, Sec. 2
Proposed 1982, S.L. page 932, H.J.R. 14, ratified November 2, 1982.

AMENDMENT No. 100, Art.V, Sec. 18
Proposed 1982, S.L. page 933, H.J.R. 15, As Amended, ratified November 2, 1982.

AMENDMENT No. 101, Art. VIII, Sec. 5
Proposed 1982, S.L. page 933, H.J.R. 17, ratified November 2, 1982.

AMENDMENT No. 102, Art. IX, Sec. 8
Proposed 1982, S.L. page 935, H.J.R. 18, ratified November 2, 1982.

AMENDMENT No. 103, Art. XV, Sec. 7
Proposed 1984, S.L. 1984, p. 689, S.J.R. 117, As Amended; ratified November 6, 1984.

AMENDMENT No. 104, Art. XVIII, Sec. 6
Proposed 1986, S.L. page 866, S.J.R. 102, ratified November 4, 1986.

AMENDMENT No. 105, Art. IV, Sec. 7
Proposed 1986, S.L. page 867, S.J.R. 107, ratified November 4, 1986.

AMENDMENT No. 106, Art. III, Secs. 2, 4 & 5
Proposed 1986, S.L. page 869, H.J.R. 4, ratified November 4, 1986.

AMENDMENT NO. 107, Art. III, Sec. 20
Proposed 1987, S.L. page 801, H.J.R. 3, ratified November 8, 1988

AMENDMENT No. 108, Art.VII, Sec. 4
Proposed 1990, S.L. page 1214, H.J.R. 14, ratified November 6, 1990

AMENDMENT No. 109, Art. III, Sec. 20
Proposed 1992 (E.S.), S.L. page 8, H.J.R. 4, ratified November 3, 1992.

AMENDMENT No. 110, Art. III, Sec. 2, Art. V, Sec. 9
Proposed 1993, S.L. page 1530, S.J.R. 105, ratified November 8, 1994.

AMENDMENT No. 111, Art.III, Sec. 23, Art. IV, Secs. 1,3,6,19, and 20, Art. V, Sec. 27, Art. IX, Sec. 7
Proposed 1994, S.L. page 1493, S.J.R. 109, ratified November 8, 1994.

AMENDMENT No. 112, Art. I, Sec. 22 ADDED
Proposed 1994, S.L. page 1498, H.J.R. 16, ratified November 8, 1994.

AMENDMENT No. 113, Art. XVIII, Sec. 12 ADDED
Proposed 1994, S.L. page 1499, H.J.R. 17, ratified November 8, 1994.

AMENDMENT No. 114, Art. IV, Sec. 1
Proposed 1994, S.L. page 1500, H.J.R. 24, ratified November 8, 1994.

AMENDMENT No. 115, Art. VIII, Sec. 3C ADDED
Proposed 1996, S.L. page 1473, S.J.R. 111, ratified November 5, 1996.

AMENDMENT No. 116, Art. V, Sec 17, Sec 27
Proposed 1997, S.L. page 1300 S.J.R. 101, ratified November 3, 1998.

AMENDMENT No. 117, Art. IV, Section 19 (repealed)
Proposed 1997, S.L. page 1301, S.J.R. 102, ratified November 3, 1998.

AMENDMENT No. 118, Art. VI, Section 3
Proposed 1998, S.L. page 1361, S.J.R. 105, ratified November 3, 1998.

AMENDMENT No. 119, Art VIII, Sec 2
Proposed 1998, S.L. page 1362, S.J. R. 106, ratified November 3, 1998.

AMENDMENT No. 120, Art. VIII, Sec 1
Proposed 1998, S.L. page 1363, S.J.R. 107, ratified November 3, 1998.

AMENDMENT No. 121, Art. IX, Secs. 4 & 8
Proposed 1998, S.L. page 1366, H.J.R. 6, ratified November 3, 1998.
RULED UNCONSTITUTIONAL By Idaho Watershed Project v. State Board of Land Commissioners 133 Id. 55, 982 P.2d 358 (1999)

AMENDMENT No. 122, Art. IX, Secs 3 & 11
Proposed 1998, S.L. page 1368, H.J.R. 8, ratified November 3, 1998.

AMENDMENT No. 123, Art. IX, Section 4
Proposed 2000, S.L. page 1669, H.J.R. 1, ratified November 7, 2000.

AMENDMENT No. 124, Art. VIII, Section 2A
Proposed 2000, S.L. page 1664, S.J.R. 107, ratified November 7, 2000.

AMENDMENT No. 125, Art. III, Section 28
Proposed 2006, S.L. page 1359, H.J.R. 2, ratified November 7, 2006.

AMENDMENT No. 126, Art. VII, Section 18
Proposed 2006, S.L. page 1356, S.J.R. 107, ratified November 7, 2006.

AMENDMENT No. 127, Art. IX, Section 10
Proposed 2009, S.L. page 1080, S.J.R. 101, ratified November 2, 2010.

AMENDMENT No. 128, Art. VIII, Section 3C
Proposed 2010, S.L. page 947, H.J.R. 4, ratified November 2, 2010.

AMENDMENT No. 129, Art. VIII, Section 3E ADDED
Proposed 2010, S.L. page 948, H.J.R. 5, ratified November 2, 2010.

AMENDMENT No. 130, Art. VIII, Section 3D ADDED
Proposed 2010, S.L. page 950, H.J.R. 7, ratified November 2, 2010.

AMENDMENT No. 131, Art. X, Section 5
Proposed 2012, S.L. page 956, S.J.R. 102, ratified November 6, 2012.

AMENDMENT No. 132, Art. I, Section 23 ADDED
Proposed 2012, S.L. page 957, H.J.R. 2, ratified November 6, 2012.

AMENDMENT No. 133, Art. III, Section 29 ADDED
Proposed 2016, S.L. page 1107, H.J.R. 5, ratified November 8, 2016.

Made in the USA
Las Vegas, NV
03 December 2022

61044473R00032